FAVORITE RECIPES

of

WHITESTONE COUNTRY INN

To him that overcometh will I give to eat of the hidden manna, and will give him a white stone, and in the stone a new name written, which no man knoweth saving he that receiveth.

Revelation 2:17

Published by William and Warren, Inc.
1200 Paint Rock Road
Kingston, Tennessee 37763
(888) 247-2464

Library of Congress Cataloging-in-Publication Data
Cowell, Jean;
     Favorite Recipes of Whitestone Country Inn
     ISBN 0-9652007-0-1
     1. Bed and Breakfast Accommodations — U.S. — Directories
     2. Food
     3. Whitestone

Dewey System — Ideas and Recipes

Photography credits: Morris Bagwell; Gary Heatherly–Knoxville; Carl Ross, Vicki Cowell

Cover and text design by Juanita Smith, Knoxville, Tennessee
Printed by Classic Printing, Nashville, Tennessee

Whitestone Country Inn is a member of *Select Registry, Tennessee Bed & Breakfast Innkeepers Association, Johansens* and the *Professional Association of Innkeepers*. It has a 4-Diamond rating from AAA. Whitestone was voted one of the ten most romantic Inns in America. Several articles have been written about Whitestone Country Inn and Paul and Jean Cowell's dream home. *HGTV* will produce a film excerpt featuring Whitestone during the summer of 2001. *Southern Living*~TM~ Magazine will feature the Inn in a special section during the fall of 2001. *Tennessee Crossroads*, a public TV show, has filmed and run a documentary of Whitestone Country Inn several times over the past years. The Chapel at Whitestone has been a focal point used by countless wedding photographers during the last three years.

Dedicated to …

Chef Dodd Orton, whose education and experience have added immensely to the culinary enjoyment at Whitestone.

In Appreciation …

Thank you to all our friends, family, chefs and employees (past and present) that have contributed recipes, support and help that have contributed to this cookbook. You have added inspiration, variety and creativity as we have developed Whitestone's "favorite" recipes.

Special appreciation goes to all the Inns we have visited and Innkeepers that have assisted and influenced us in Whitestone's beginning days. Many of them have given us recipes, ideas and encouragement as we have developed our identity.

We also want to thank those who did data entry and proof reading. Graphic designer, Juanita Smith, has spent many hours doing the layout and design work. Her help and friendship has been invaluable.

Most of all, we thank our Whitestone guests for their comments, suggestions and encouragement. They have been our recipe testers. Without you, this book would not exist.

God bless you all!

Paul Cowell   Jean Cowell

The White&Stone Story…

The Vision

In August, 1963, Paul and Jean vacationed for a week at a resort in upstate New York. The accommodations were rustic; but the peaceful setting on the shores of an Adirondack lake provided a wonderful time of inspiration and recreation.

Paul spent an afternoon sitting in the resort's chapel writing out his vision for a similar retreat on one of the lakes in East Tennessee. That dream changed through the years as his experience refined his desire to provide a special peaceful escape.

As a pastor, much of the marriage counseling Paul did led him to the conclusion that a lot of people just need a good night's sleep and someone else to fix them breakfast. The dream for a place of real tranquility grew in Paul's heart. He and Jean began to measure hotel rooms, visit country resorts and make plans.

Purchase of Property

Dozens of properties were visited in the years following. Paul and Jean often toured distressed resorts and farms, looking for an affordable site. In 1981 an option was taken on 260 acres on Norris Lake. After extensive planning and analysis, this site was rejected by Paul and the other investors.

After over 20 years of evaluating potential sites, Paul visited the 275 acres that is now "Whitestone" with a Knoxville realtor in 1989. The property was densely wooded with pine trees and undergrowth. Several hikes up and down the hills and through the thickets convinced Paul that the property had all the components required for a spectacular resort. The Cowells took an option from the owner, Glen Hill of Rockwood. Glen had purchased the land in 1987.

Over a year was spent in acquiring surveys and building table sized models of the property. Little wooden buildings were moved around the table model. The dream was becoming clearer. Hours were consumed walking the hills and

shoreline. In 1991, the decision was finalized to acquire the property.

Schedule of Development

In 1939, TVA had planted pine trees on the cleared farmland that is now Whitestone. A logging company was given a contract to cut the pine but leave the hardwood in January, 1994. Three months of this activity left a war zone effect.

Two bulldozers then worked every day for almost six months (March - July, 94) pushing up stumps and windrowing brush and debris for burning. Paul drove down from Knoxville almost every day with a crew to facilitate the clean up. Months were spent picking up

rocks and burning brush. Paul
and un-paid friends dedicated
themselves to turning a pine forest
into pasture and lawn.

With the views opened for the
first time by the logging activity,
revisions were made in the
master plan. The individual
component pieces remained the
same but placement was changed
to maximize views.

The Cowells house in Knoxville
was listed for sale in August, 1995. Paul left for a speaking trip to West Africa. A fax was
waiting at the hotel when he arrived,
informing him that the house had
sold. (He thinks he must have priced
it too low!)

What should have been an orderly
transition to Paint Rock Road took
on frenzied proportions. The plans for
the "drive through entrance barn"
were hurriedly completed by
Architect Gary Best of
Maryville. In the first week of
September, 1995, construction was started on the 4,000 square foot, four

unit entrance barn. Paul and Jean moved in on December 3, to what is now the Meadowlark Suite. Moving from 3200 square feet to 672 square feet was a "we don't need that! Throw it away!" challenge. Ken and Debbie Warren from Columbus, Ohio, occupied the second floor apartment and were a real blessing in the next year of development.

The vision was taking shape!

Building the Farmhouse

All of 1996 was spent planning and building the big farmhouse. Nine bedrooms and suites, kitchens, great room, recreation room, conference room, two dining areas, library, laundries, etc. — 15,000 square feet of functional bed and breakfast living.

Jean took charge of decorating. Bird names were selected. Everything was planned to make the guests feel comfortable — colors, window treatments, furniture and artwork.

Paul supervised the daily construction. Delbert Roberts and his crew of carpenters started in March with a completion goal of December. Paul and Jean moved into the Mallard suite on December 15, 1996.

The Warrens left in November and returned to Ohio. Jean's aunt and uncle, Dave and Dottie Strepka, moved into the Sparrow suite in the barn. Dave was the first chef. Dottie does all the flower arranging for the Inn and assists Jean with the decorating.

Jean's family came for Christmas 1996 to be sure everything functioned as it should. Whitestone had two buildings with a total of twelve rooms. The first paying guest arrived the first week in January, 1997. A 34-year dream became reality! (And it was better than the dream.)

Personal Background

Until January, 1994, Paul and Jean remained deeply involved in activities in Knoxville. Beginning in 1985 with one bookstore in Knoxville, the Cowells operated 62 wholly owned bookstores and 33 licensed bookstores by 1992. The stores were sold in 1992-93.

Paul had bought controlling interest in a home shopping network in 1988. This small TV network grew dramatically in the next five years. Paul resigned as Chairman of the Board of Shop At Home Inc. at the end of 1993, to devote himself to the Whitestone development.

During this time, Paul and Jean also pastored an interdenominational church in Knoxville. He had founded the church in 1963 and pastored it until 1983. He then returned to the pastorate there in 1989. They resigned in December, 1994, as part of their preparation for moving to the Inn.

The Little Red Schoolhouse

The master plan called for Whitestone when completed, to look like an eclectic New England village—a rambling collection of village buildings in a self-contained setting. In 1998, construction was completed on a replica of a country schoolhouse.

A gift shop, offices and two guest suites occupy the first and second floor. The full basement provides much needed storage space.

Paul and Jean's son, Kevin, and his wife, Vicki, moved into the Chickadee suite in October, '96. They built a nice log home on the property and moved to it in May, '98. Vicki operates the gift shop and does much of the purchasing for the Inn. Kevin's accounting office is in the Schoolhouse. He and Vicki assist in all aspects of daily operations. Grandchildren, Dakota and Cheyenne, add joy to everyone's life.

The Rose Cottage

The Rose Cottage was completed in January of 2000. There are two luxurious rooms, the Mockingbird on the first floor and the Oriole on the second. Each has a private deck right on the bluff above the lake. Winter views are especially good from this vantage point.

By the summer of 2000, there were 20 rooms in five different buildings.

Chapel Hill

Construction began in October 1998, on the last large building project at Whitestone.

"Chapel Hill" is the highest point on the property with incredible lake, island and mountain views. A 175-seat chapel with a large Victorian house next door had been conceived as part of the original master plan.

The chapel is an expanded replica of the Anglican Church in Rugby, Tennessee. Rugby was a utopian 1800's village built by an Englishman, Thomas Hughes. The chapel at Whitestone is perfectly proportioned to embody the quintessential country chapel.

The Lion and The Lamb adjacent to the chapel provides a 175-seat dining room with wrap-around porches. Upstairs there are three luxurious suites and a state-of-the-art conference room that will accommodate 50.

Chapel Hill is the perfect setting for a gas lit, heart shaped marble courtyard and gazebo. Weddings are conducted both in the chapel and outside on the courtyard.

Activity and Inactivity Abound

Many guests come to the inn with nothing on the agenda but a quiet room, good food, comfortable decks and porches, rocking chairs and rest. Others find the energy for canoes, paddleboats, tennis, croquet and horseshoes. Eight miles of trails through woods and beside the lake provide ample on-site hiking and bird watching opportunities for those so inclined.

The recreation room has a pool table, ping-pong table, board games and exercise equipment for additional entertainment.

Fireplaces, spa tubs and quiet spacious rooms with televisions and vcr's give those seeking retreat a place of their own.

Keeping the Guests Happy

The air conditioner froze in the Cardinal room. (The large suite at the top of the stairs above the kitchen.) A smell of burnt insulation was easily detectable when housekeeping entered the room to prepare it for the overnight guests checking in. Candles and incense were burned, vinegar was put out, air fresheners were plugged in and all windows and doors were opened. By 3:00 pm, the smell was hardly detectable. Maybe just a faint hint of burnt something.

The arriving guests were pleased with the room and enthusiastic about their stay.

Nothing was mentioned at check-in or at dinner about any lingering smell.

Thirty minutes before breakfast the next morning one of the guests in the Cardinal came down the stairs. "Good morning. How did you sleep?" Paul asked in his cheery best.

"How do you think I slept with the smell up there!" the man exclaimed. Just before Paul could offer apologies and the room free, the guest continued on, "coffee, bacon, biscuits, muffins — you can smell it all up there! I'm ready for breakfast!"

Neither party ever mentioned the burnt insulation smell.

Paul's Foot in His Mouth…

Lunch was being served. The sunroom was filled to capacity as the hum of pleasant conversation mingled with the click of silverware and glasses.

"How was your food?" Paul asked two couples at a round table by the window. "It was very good" was the courteous response from one of the gentlemen. Paul continued by saying, "We're not real fancy. We're just trying to serve good American food."

"Well it is great country cooking," the guest responded.

"Our mission statement regarding food is to be a little better than the Cracker Barrel," Paul quipped.

At that point both couples began to laugh. As they continued to laugh, Paul asked, "Are we not better than the Cracker Barrel?" Finally one of the men smiled and replied, "I'm one of the founders of Cracker Barrel."

After Paul removed his foot from his mouth and the laughter subsided, he was given permission to continue to use that as a mission statement. The guests returned for a weekend stay and have become friends.

Why?

The most often asked question by guests at Whitestone is "What led you to decide to do this?" Paul and Jean believe they were placed on earth to be productive. They get deep satisfaction by serving others. Surely we are supposed to lighten the load of others and make the world a better place.

America has been duplicating and franchising for so long that there are too few unique places or memorable experiences remaining. The goal at Whitestone is to create (with God's help) a retreat that could provide true sanctuary for the soul. We can be so busy and stressed by our daily lives that we forget to listen to the still small voice inside that can only be heard when the clatter of the world is silenced.

The "Whitestone Experience" is designed to help each guest slow down and reconnect to the center of his or her existence. The facilities, amenities, staff and dining experience are all planned to provide an unhurried leisure pace.

The goal is for Whitestone to feel like home. One of the frequent guests said it best, "Whitestone is the only place I've ever been homesick for other than home." (Bobby Scobey)

The "Whitestone Experience" is elegant but unpretentious; friendly but not hovering; and the food is excellent but recognizable.

Most importantly Whitestone exists because of a calling. "It's a great way to spend our brief time on earth….loving the things and people God sent us here to love."

Contents

The Chapel, butterfly bushes & stained glass window, ask Paul to tell you the story…

Relax in one of our famous hideaways…

Come for an autumn hayride…

Celebrate with us for a 4th of July buffet…

Winter splendor around the barn…

Take a boat ride & look at the views…

Harvest time at Whitestone…

FAVORITE RECIPES of WHITESTONE COUNTRY INN

Appetizers

...A gorgeous, spacious and truly peaceful atmosphere. ...Thank you for such a magnificent complex, combined with God's nature for a setting that is unforgettable.

Bacon Wraps

Preheat to 350°...

Amt Measure	Ingredient — Preparation Method
1 package	*bacon slices*
1 can	*pineapple chunks — drained*

Cut bacon strips in half. Place one pineapple chunk on the end of the bacon slice and roll up.

Place on an ungreased baking sheet seam side down.

Bake at 350° until bacon has browned then remove from oven and flip all pieces and bake until done.

NOTES:

Serve 4 or 5 of these for appetizers.

You can also wrap water chestnuts, scallops, shrimp or chicken livers.

Sprinkle top of bacon with brown sugar for a nice flavor.

Beggar's Pockets or Parcels

Servings: 8 • Preheat to 400°...

Melt butter in large non-stick skillet.

Add leeks and cook over medium heat until soft then transfer to bowl and cool.

Stir in cheese, tomatoes and pepper and sprinkle with a dash of salt.

Lay one pastry on counter. Brush with butter and fold in half. Brush again with butter then fold once more in half. This will give you four folds.

Place one tablespoon of leeks and cheese mixture in center of pastry brushing edges of pastry with butter. Then pull up corners to seal the filling and place on sheet pan. Repeat until all pastry and filling is used.

Bake 10 minutes at 400°.

Amt Measure	Ingredient — Preparation Method
2 tablespoons	unsalted butter
8 ounces	trimmed leeks or baby spinach
4 ounces	goat cheese or cream cheese
2 ounces	sun-dried tomatoes — finely chopped
	fresh ground pepper & salt to taste
8 sheets	phyllo pastry
	melted butter for brushing

NOTE:

Serve warm.

Japanese Marinated Mushrooms

Servings: 8

Amt Measure	Ingredient — Preparation Method
2 pounds	mushrooms (your choice)
1/4 cup	soy sauce
1/2 cup	sweet sherry
1/2 cup	white vinegar
1 1/2 teaspoons	salt
1/2 cup	onion — minced

Cook cleaned, fresh mushrooms in boiling water for 7 minutes.

Drain water from mushrooms and put mushrooms in a glass container.

In a sauce pan, bring soy sauce, sherry, vinegar, salt and onion to a boil.

Pour mixture over the mushrooms, cover and refrigerate for at least 24 hours.

Mushroom en Croute

Servings: 8 • Preheat to 400°...

Amt Measure	Ingredient — Preparation Method
1 cup	garlic & herb soft cheese
24 even sized	mushrooms — stems removed
12 sheets	phyllo pastry
1 cup	butter — melted
	salt to taste
	fresh ground black pepper to taste
1	egg — beaten with 1 tablespoon water

Peel mushrooms and stuff each with cheese.

Brush with melted butter and stack four phyllo sheets then cut into eight squares.

Wrap one mushroom in each square. Repeat until all mushrooms are wrapped.

Salt and pepper to taste.

Brush with egg and bake on baking sheet about 12 to 15 minutes until golden and crisp.

NOTE:
Serves three to each person.

Pecan-Crusted Artichoke & Cheese Spread

Servings: 16 • Preheat to 350°...

Amt Measure	Ingredient — Preparation Method
1/4 cup	butter — divided
1 medium	onion — diced
2 cloves	garlic bulbs — minced
4 cups	fresh spinach — chopped
13 3/4 ounces	canned artichoke hearts — chopped
1/2 cup	mayonnaise
8 ounces	cream cheese — cut into chunks
3/4 cup	Parmesan cheese — shredded
8 ounces	four cheese blend
2/3 cup	pecans — chopped
1/2 cup	herb-seasoned stuffing mix

Melt three tablespoons butter in a large skillet; add onion and garlic and saute until tender.

Add spinach and cook over medium heat, stirring often for three minutes.

Add artichoke hearts, mayonnaise, cream cheese, Parmesan cheese and cheese blend, stirring until cheeses have melted.

Spoon into a greased 2 quart baking dish.

Bake for 20 minutes; stir gently.

Combine remaining butter, pecans and stuffing mix in a bowl, toss until blended.

Sprinkle over top and bake 15 additional minutes.

NOTES:

You can also use small phyllo dough cups for individual servings. Serve this dip with toasted pita bread wedges or cocktail bread. For the "four cheese blend" you can substitute any assortment of shredded cheeses.

Phyllo Star Clusters with Caramelized Onions

Servings: 8 • Preheat to 350°...

Sauté onions with four tablespoons butter until caramelized. Do not burn.

Add mushrooms, red peppers, olives and salt. Cook until warm. Set aside to cool.

In blender mix cheese, garlic and herbs until soft and spreadable.

Layer one phyllo sheet. Brush with butter.

Repeat until you have four sheets stacked. Cut into four squares.

Put one teaspoon onion mixture and one teaspoon cheese mixture on each square of phyllo. Pull up corners and twist to seal.

Bake on sheet pan lined with parchment paper for 15 to 20 minutes or until golden brown.

Amt Measure	Ingredient — Preparation Method
3 cups	onions — coarsely chopped
4 tablespoons	butter
1 1/2 cups	mushrooms — chopped
2/3 cup	roasted red peppers — chopped
1/4 cup	pitted black olives — chopped
1/4 teaspoon	salt
1 cup	cream cheese or mascarpone cheese — softened
1 teaspoon	garlic — chopped fine
2 tablespoons	fresh herbs, chives, dill & thyme
8 sheets	phyllo pastry — thawed
1/2 cup	melted butter

Pickled Shrimp Marinade

Servings: 6

Amt Measure	Ingredient — Preparation Method
1 1/2 pounds	large shrimp — 20-26 count
1 cup	water
1 cup	malt vinegar
1/2 cup	oil
1/2 cup	lime juice
2 tablespoons	sugar
2 tablespoons	kosher salt
3	bay leaves (Turkey leaves)
1 1/2 teaspoons	black pepper
1 teaspoon	dill seed
1 teaspoon	celery seed
1 teaspoon	dry mustard
1/2 teaspoon	dried tarragon — crushed fine
1/4 teaspoon	cayenne pepper
1/4 teaspoon	Tabasco sauce
2 medium	onions — sliced paper-thin

Boil shrimp in pot of salted water for two or three minutes. Remove from water and pack in ice water to stop cooking.

Mix all other ingredients except onions in stock pot, simmer uncovered for five minutes.

Using a four quart bowl, place a thin layer of onions in bottom of bowl.

Put a layer of shrimp on top of onions and continue layering until ingredients are all gone. Be sure to finish with a layer of onions.

Pour marinade over top. Cover with plastic wrap. Place a plate with two or three pounds. of weight on top of bowl. Marinade for 12 hours.

Stir and mix before serving.

NOTE:
Serve the shrimp with a slice or two of onion on party rye bread.

Pinwheels

Servings: 12

Mix cream cheese, salad dressing, olives, celery, green onions and red peppers until smooth.

Divide into four equal portions.

Spread one portion on each tortilla. Roll tightly and wrap individually in plastic wrap.

Refrigerate two hours. Slice into 1/2 inch thick pinwheels.

Garnish with parsley in center of each.

NOTE:

Makes four dozen pinwheels. Serve four or five for an appetizer.

Amt Measure	Ingredient — Preparation Method
8 ounces	cream cheese
1 envelope	ranch cracked pepper salad dressing
1/2 cup	stuffed olives — sliced
1/2 cup	celery — chopped fine
1/4 cup	green onions — chopped fine
1/4 cup	red peppers — chopped fine
4	tortilla burritos (refrigerator section)
	parsley for garnish

Stuffed Mushrooms

Servings: 30   •   Preheat to 350°...

Amt Measure	Ingredient — Preparation Method
4 tablespoons	*Parmesan cheese — grated*
8 ounces	*cream cheese*
4 ounces	*crabmeat or sausage*
2 1/2 tablespoons	*olive oil*
2 tablespoons	*fresh parsley — chopped*
1 1/2 tablespoons	*bread crumbs*
	juice of 1/2 lemon
1 1/2 teaspoons	*shallot — minced*
1 teaspoon	*Dijon mustard*
1 teaspoon	*salt*
1/2 teaspoon	*fresh ground pepper*
30 approximately	*mushrooms — stems removed*
	garlic butter for brushing
1 1/2 teaspoons	*cognac, brandy or white wine for brushing*
	fresh parsley for garnish

In bowl, mix two tablespoons Parmesan cheese and the next ten ingredients (to the mushrooms).

Beat 5 to 10 minutes.

Stuff mushrooms and sprinkle with remaining Parmesan cheese.

Brush with cognac and garlic butter.

Bake 10 minutes.

Garnish with fresh parsley.

NOTE:
Stuffing will keep in refrigerator for three or four days.

Beverages

. . . We have seen few places which truly capture the beauty of
its surroundings as Whitestone has so gracefully achieved.
This stay has been a splendid experience which followed the
wedding of our dreams. . . .

Bride's Pink Punch

Servings: 36

Amt Measure	Ingredient — Preparation Method
3 ounces	strawberry jello
1 cup	boiling water
1 package	strawberry powdered drink mix
2 cups	sugar
2 quarts	water
46 ounces	pineapple juice (unsweetened)
10 ounces	7-Up®
1 quart	pineapple sherbet

Dissolve jello in boiling water. Add all other ingredients except the 7-Up® and sherbet.

Chill until serving time.

Add 7-Up® at serving time.

Put sherbet in punch bowl and pour punch over the sherbet.

Evergreen Punch

Servings: 36

Dissolve sugar in the water.

Add drink mix and juice.

Chill until serving time.

Add ginger ale at serving time.

Put sherbet in punch bowl and pour punch over sherbet.

Amt Measure	Ingredient — Preparation Method
2 cups	sugar
2 quarts	water
2 packages	lime powdered drink mix
46 ounces	pineapple juice
1 quart	ginger ale
1 quart	lime sherbet

Holiday Egg Nog

Servings: 20

Amt Measure	Ingredient — Preparation Method
1 quart	*sugar*
15	*eggs*
1 quart	*milk*
1 tablespoon	*cinnamon*
1 tablespoon	*nutmeg*
1 teaspoon	*cloves — ground*
1 quart	*whipping cream — whipped*

Whip sugar, eggs and milk together on high for 15 minutes.

Heat to 140° on stove.

Cool and add the remaining ingredients.

Beat until well blended and foamy.

Serve immediately.

NOTES:

This fills a large punch bowl and is delicious! Use your leftover egg nog to make wonderful French toast.

Mock Champagne

Servings: 24

Chill juice and ginger ale. Combine just before serving.

Amt Measure	Ingredient — Preparation Method
2 64-ounce bottles	white grape juice
2 2-litre bottles	ginger ale

Serving Ideas:
In fall, freeze whole pieces of fall fruit and float in punch bowl.
In summer, make a frozen fruit ring or float strawberries.

Mock Pink Champagne

Servings: 14

Bring water to a boil and stir in sugar until dissolved. Cool.

Stir in the juices. Chill.

Before serving add the lemon-lime carbonated beverage.

Amt Measure	Ingredient — Preparation Method
1 1/2 cups	water
1/2 cup	sugar
2 cups	cranberry juice
1 cup	pineapple juice
1/2 cup	orange juice
14 ounces	lemon-lime carbonated beverage

FAVORITE RECIPES of WHITESTONE COUNTRY INN

Bread

The beauty of this place is beyond what words can express. It gave our group a chance to learn more about each other in a calm atmosphere. We walked near the water, played croquet for the first time and enjoyed the room thoroughly. God allows us a little bit of Heaven on earth and I believe God has allowed us to have this haven for reflection this week. Thank you so much for your hospitality.

Bacon Fry Bread

Servings: 16 • Preheat oven to 350°...

Amt Measure	Ingredient — Preparation Method
1 pound	bacon slices
4	eggs
1 cup	milk
2 cups	all-purpose flour
1 tablespoon	sugar
2 1/2 teaspoons	baking powder
1 1/2 teaspoons	salt

Place bacon in oven for 15 to 20 minutes or until golden. Drain saving the drippings. Coarsely chop bacon.

Mix eggs, milk, one cup flour, sugar, baking powder and salt. Beat until smooth. Add remaining flour and beat until smooth.

Using a 10" skillet, add 1 tablespoon of bacon drippings and half of the bacon. Then add half of the batter and cook on medium heat (on stove top) until batter starts to set and brown.

Flip over the cake and cook until batter starts to set. Place on baking sheet.

Repeat with remaining bacon and batter.

Bake for 30 minutes until golden. Test for doneness with cake tester.

Cut into wedges for serving.

NOTES:

We found this recipe in an old Polish cookbook. At Whitestone we serve this with our salad course. It is always a hit.

Cheddar Cheese & Onion Bread

Yield: 1 flower pot • Preheat oven to 350°...

Grease small bread pan or clay flower pot.

In a mixing bowl mix flour, salt, sugar, baking powder and dried onions.

Add melted butter, milk and cheese and mix with spoon until well blended.

Add the egg and mix thoroughly.

Bake for 40 to 50 minutes until a toothpick inserted in center comes out clean. Cool at least 10 minutes before serving.

Amt Measure	Ingredient — Preparation Method
2/3 cup	all-purpose flour
1/4 teaspoon	salt
1/4 cup	sugar
1 teaspoon	baking powder
1 teaspoon	dried onion
1 tablespoon	butter
2 tablespoons	milk
1/4 cup	cheddar cheese — grated
1	egg — lightly beaten

NOTES:

We use clay flower pots that have a glazed coating in them. You can find these at kitchen supply stores. Small loaf pans can also be used.

Crescent Rolls

Servings: 24 • Preheat to 350°...

Amt Measure	Ingredient — Preparation Method
1 package	yeast
1/4 cup	warm water — 110°
1 cup	scalded milk
1/4 cup	shortening
1/4 cup	sugar
1 teaspoon	salt
1	egg — beaten
3 1/2 cups	bread flour
	melted butter for brushing surfaces

Dissolve yeast in the water. Combine milk, shortening, sugar, salt and egg. Mix well.

Add the flour and beat at a high speed.

Cover and let rise for one hour.

Divide dough into three balls. Roll out ball and brush butter over surface.

Cut into 12 wedges and roll each piece from big end to little end.

Allow the rolls to rise for one hour and bake for 10 to 15 minutes or until golden brown.

Brush with butter while rolls are still hot.

Croutons

Preheat to 400°...

Toss cubed bread with butter, garlic salt and cheese.

Bake until brown. Stir occasionally to brown evenly.

Amt Measure	Ingredient — Preparation Method
1 loaf	French bread — 1 inch cubes
1 cup	butter — melted
2 tablespoons	garlic salt
4 tablespoons	Parmesan cheese — grated

NOTES:

Store in air tight container.

For variety, try various kinds of bread.

Hard Rolls

Servings: 36 • Preheat to 350°...

Amt Measure	Ingredient — Preparation Method
1 quart	water — 105°
4 ounces	yeast
2 ounces	milk powder
1 ounce	salt
1 ounce	shortening
1 ounce	sugar
3 1/2 pounds	bread flour
	olive oil for brushing

Combine all ingredients except flour in mixing bowl and let stand for 8 to 10 minutes until yeast bubbles. Add flour.

Mix on low speed five minutes then mix at medium speed for 6-8 minutes. Dough should pull away from bowl.

Brush the bowl and dough with shortening and let rise until it doubles in bulk.

Punch down dough and shape into rolls or french bread loaves.

Let rise again until doubles in bulk and bake for 15 to 20 minutes.

Brush with olive oil while hot.

NOTES:

This can also be used to make French Bread. For bread loaves bake at 400° for 20 to 30 minutes.

Italian Herb Bread

Yield: 1 flower pot • Preheat to 350°...

Amt Measure	Ingredient — Preparation Method
2/3 cup	all-purpose flour
1/4 teaspoon	salt
1/4 cup	sugar
1 teaspoon	baking powder
1/2 teaspoon	Italian seasoning
1 tablespoon	butter
2 tablespoons	milk
1/4 cup	tomatoes — finely chopped
1	egg — beaten lightly

Coat small bread pan or one flowerpot with vegetable spray.

In a large bowl, mix flour, salt, sugar, baking powder and Italian seasoning.

Add butter, milk, tomatoes and egg.

Pour batter into flower pot or loaf pan and bake for 40 to 50 minutes.

The bread is done when a toothpick inserted in the center comes out clean. Cool for 10 minutes before serving.

NOTES:
We use clay flower pots that have a glazed coating in them. You can find these at kitchen supply stores. Small loaf pans can also be used.

Jalapeno Cornbread

Servings: 8 • Preheat to 350°...

Amt Measure	Ingredient — Preparation Method
1 1/2 cups	yellow cornmeal
3 teaspoons	baking powder
1 teaspoon	salt
1 large	jalapeno pepper — diced
1 can	cream style corn
1/2 cup	cooking oil
2	eggs
8 ounces	sour cream
1 1/2 cups	grated cheddar cheese

Mix all of the above ingredients except the cheese.

Pour half of the mixture into a hot oiled cast iron skillet.

Sprinkle the cheese on top of the mixture and pour the remaining mixture over the cheese.

Bake for 45 minutes or until brown.

Cheddar Cheese Biscuits

Servings: 24 • Preheat to 350°...

Mix flour and shortening until it resembles cornmeal, then add buttermilk and cheese.

Mix just until blended. *Do Not Overmix*.

Turn out on floured surface. Knead 5 or 6 times.

Roll out to 3/4" thick and cut with small biscuit cutter.

Bake for 15 to 20 minutes.

Amt Measure	Ingredient — Preparation Method
2 cups	self-rising flour
1/3 cup	shortening
1 cup	buttermilk
1 cup	cheddar cheese — shredded

NOTES:
Makes two dozen mini-biscuits.
Serve with soup or salad.

Parker House Rolls

Servings: 24 • Preheat to 400°...

Amt Measure	Ingredient — Preparation Method
2 tablespoons	shortening
1 teaspoon	salt
1/4 cup	sugar
2 tablespoons	yeast
1 1/2 cups	water — Heat to 105°
3 1/2 cups	all-purpose flour — sifted
1	egg — beaten
	butter — melted

Add shortening, salt, sugar and yeast to water. Stir until shortening is melted.

Stir in flour and mix until well blended. Let rise in warm place until doubled in bulk.

Add egg, then knead lightly, let rise again.

Roll out to 1/2" thick. Cut with 2-inch cutter.

Crease center and brush with melted butter. fold over, pinching at sides to look like a pocket book.

Place on baking sheet and brush with butter. Let rise until doubles.

Bake 18 to 20 minutes or until golden brown.

Soft Dinner Rolls

Servings: 36 • Preheat to 350°...

Water temperature should be no more than 110°.

In a mixer combine all ingredients except for the flour. Let stand for 10 minutes undisturbed.

Add the flour and mix on low speed for 6 minutes. Then mix on medium speed for 6 minutes or until the dough leaves the side of the bowl.

Rub the bowl and dough with shortening and let rise for 1 1/2 hours or until doubled.

Roll out rolls in desired shapes and let rise for 1 1/2 hours.

Bake for 10 to 15 minutes or until golden brown. Brush with butter while hot.

Amt Measure	Ingredient — Preparation Method
1 quart	warm water
4 ounces	yeast
4 ounces	milk powder
2 ounces	salt
6 ounces	sugar
6 ounces	shortening
3 1/2 pounds	bread flour
	butter melted for brushing

Sourdough Bread

Preheat to 400°...

Amt Measure	Ingredient — Preparation Method
4 teaspoons	dry yeast
1 1/2 cups	warm water
5 1/2 cups	all-purpose flour
1 cup	sourdough starter
2 teaspoons	sugar
1 teaspoon	salt
1/2 teaspoon	baking soda
1	egg — beaten
1 teaspoon	water

Sourdough Starter:

4 teaspoons	dry yeast
1/2 cup	warm water
2 cups	all-purpose flour
1 tablespoon	sugar
3/4 cup	water
3/4 cup	all-purpose flour
1 tablespoon	sugar

In bowl soften yeast in warm water. Blend in 2 1/2 cups flour, sourdough starter at room temperature, sugar and salt. Mix 2 1/2 cups flour with soda. Stir into mixture. Add enough remaining flour to make stiff dough. Knead until smooth. Place in greased bowl, cover and let rise until double in bulk. Punch down. Let rest 10 or 15 minutes. Shape into loaves or 1 1/2 ounce rolls. Cut slashes on top. Let rise until double in bulk. Bake 35 to 40 minutes or until golden brown. Ten minutes before it is done baking, brush with egg wash using 1 beaten egg and 1 teaspoon water.

Sourdough Starter:

Soften the yeast in warm water. Add 2 cups flour and 1 tablespoon sugar and stir together. Place in plastic bowl. Cover with cheese cloth. Let stand 5 to 10 days stirring 2 to 3 times a day. Cover and refrigerate until ready to use. After using, add 3/4 cups water, 3/4 cups flour and 1 tablespoon sugar. Let stand at room temperature one day then refrigerate. If not used, add 1 tablespoon sugar every 10 days.

NOTE:
Makes 2 small loaves.

Spoon Rolls

Servings: 24 • Preheat to 400°...

Dissolve yeast in warm water.
Add remaining ingredients and mix
well. (Add flour a little at a time
mixing between each addition).

Store covered in refrigerator for
up to 2 to 3 days.

Grease muffin tins and fill 2/3 full.
(We use an ice cream scoop.)

Allow to rise at least 30 minutes
before baking.

Bake for 15 minutes or until golden
brown.

Amt Measure	Ingredient — Preparation Method
2 tablespoons	yeast
4 cups	water — warmed
1/2 cup	sugar
1 1/2 cups	shortening — melted
2	eggs
8 cups	self-rising flour

NOTES:

We have used this batter to make coffee cakes and
sweet rolls. Be sure batter is made up the night
before to make it easier to manage.

Tennessee Pumpkin Bread

Servings: 12 • Preheat to 350°...

Amt Measure	Ingredient — Preparation Method
3 cups	sugar
1 cup	corn oil
4	eggs — beaten
1 pound	canned pumpkin
3 1/2 cups	all-purpose flour
1 teaspoon	baking powder
2 teaspoons	baking soda
2 teaspoons	salt
1/2 teaspoon	cloves
1 teaspoon	cinnamon
1 teaspoon	nutmeg
1 teaspoon	allspice
1/2 teaspoon	vanilla
2/3 cup	water

Combine sugar, oil and eggs. Add pumpkin.

Sift together flour, baking powder, soda and salt. Add spices.

Combine the two mixtures. Add water and vanilla.

Pour into two greased and floured loaf pans.

Bake for 1 hour or until bread tests done.

Yield: "2 loaves"

Serving Idea : Serve with honey cream cheese.

NOTE:
These freeze wonderfully!

Whitestone

Breakfasts

His love greets us every morning
with new blessings for the day;
with each sunrise, we embrace
the grace of God.
Ever mindful of his providence,
his never-failing care for us,
we celebrate the greatness of our God.

Blueberry Stuffed French Toast

Servings: 8 • Preheat to 350°...

Amt Measure	Ingredient — Preparation Method
6 slices	Texas toast
8 ounces	cream cheese
2 cups	blueberries, (frozen or fresh)
5	eggs
1/3 cup	maple syrup
1 cup	milk

Sauce:

1 cup	water
1 cup	sugar
2 tablespoons	cornstarch
2 cups	blueberries
2 tablespoons	butter — melted
	lemon slices to garnish

Remove the crust from the bread and cube.

Spray the bottom of a 9"x13" glass baking dish with vegetable spray. Place half the cubes of bread in pan.

Cube the cream cheese and put on top of the bread. Distribute blueberries over the cream cheese. Place remaining bread over the blueberries.

Beat the eggs, add the maple syrup and the milk. Pour mixture over bread and cheese.

Place plastic wrap over dish and refrigerate overnight. In the morning, remove plastic wrap and place aluminum foil over the dish.

Bake for 30 minutes. Remove the foil and bake for an additional 30 minutes.

Sauce:

Cook the water, sugar, cornstarch and 1 cup of blueberries until it thickens.

Then add one more cup of blueberries and the butter. Pour over individual pieces, garnish with lemon slices and serve.

NOTE:
It is best if you let the French toast stand for 10 minutes before cutting.

Breakfast Souffle

Servings: 8 • Preheat to 350°...

Cook sausage over medium heat until done, then drain well.

Combine sausage with remaining ingredients and mix well.

Pour into a well greased 13"x9" baking pan and refrigerate covered overnight.

Bake for one hour until set.

Amt Measure	Ingredient — Preparation Method
1 1/2 pounds	pork sausage
9	eggs
1 1/2 teaspoons	dry mustard
3 cups	milk
1 teaspoon	salt
3 slices	bread (cut into 1/4" cubes)
1 1/2 cups	shredded cheddar cheese
1 medium	onion — diced

Egg Frizzle

Servings: 4

Amt Measure	Ingredient — Preparation Method
1 tablespoon	butter
1/4 pound	chipped beef
4 teaspoons	buckwheat flour
4	eggs — beaten
1/8 teaspoon	pepper
1/4 cup	milk

Cook dried beef in butter until crisp.

Combine buckwheat, eggs, pepper and milk and mix well.

Pour into skillet over beef and scramble until done.

Garnish with orange slice and parsley.

German Egg Casserole and Red Pepper Sauce

Servings: 8 • Preheat to 400°...

Melt the butter and pour into a 9"x13" baking pan, making sure that the bottom of the pan is coated.

In a large bowl, beat the eggs slightly and stir in the cheeses.

In a separate bowl, combine the flour with the baking powder and mix with chopped ham.

Combine both mixtures. Pour into the baking pan.

Bake at 400° for 30 minutes.

Reduce heat to 350°, cover pan and bake another 30 minutes.

Casserole should be firm but not too wet or too dry.

Cut into squares and serve.

Sauce:

Peel, core, seed and cut peppers into 1/2 inch strips. Combine all ingredients in a food processor and puree. Serve on top of the eggs.

Amt Measure	Ingredient — Preparation Method
1/2 cup	butter
12	eggs
1 pound	Monterey jack cheese — grated
1 pint	cottage cheese — small curd
1/2 cup	all-purpose flour
1 teaspoon	baking powder
2 cups	ham — finely chopped (optional)

Sauce:

4 large	red bell peppers
2 tablespoons	olive oil
2 cloves	garlic — minced

NOTES:

Every oven bakes differently so watch this dish and adjust baking time accordingly. Our chef cuts into the center to check doneness.

Goldenrod Eggs

Servings: 6

Amt Measure	Ingredient — Preparation Method
8	*eggs — hard boiled*
4 tablespoons	*all-purpose flour*
1 cup	*butter — melted*
1 quart	*cream*
	fresh parsley for garnish

Peel eggs and cut in half. Separate yolks from the whites.

Chop egg whites. Press egg yolks through a fine sieve.

To make cream sauce, melt butter and stir in flour until bubbling. Add cream and cook until thick.

Stir egg whites into sauce.

To serve, spoon cream mixture into sauce boat and sprinkle egg yolks on top. Garnish with toast points and fresh parsley.

NOTE:
This is also good served over whole grain toast.

Poached Eggs on Potato Cakes

Servings: 8

Pare and boil potatoes until tender. Mash and add butter, cheese, salt and pepper.

Shape into cakes and fry until golden.

Prepare a sauce by browning the onions in the oil from frying the potatoes. Add tomatoes and simmer about 20 minutes.

Cover potato cakes with sauce and top with a poached egg.

Garnish with chopped parsley.

Amt Measure	Ingredient — Preparation Method
4 large	potatoes
2 tablespoons	butter
2 tablespoons	cheese — grated
	salt and pepper to taste
	butter for frying potatoes — melted
2	onions — sliced
3	tomatoes — sliced
6	eggs — poached
	parsley chopped for garnish

Quiche Lorraine

Servings: 8 • Preheat oven to 400°...

Amt Measure	Ingredient — Preparation Method
1	9-inch pie shell — unbaked
8 slices	bacon — fried and crumbled
6 ounces	Swiss cheese — grated
3	eggs
1 1/2 cups	light cream
1/2 teaspoon	salt
1/2 teaspoon	nutmeg
1/2 teaspoon	black pepper
10 ounces	frozen spinach — chopped and drained
1/4 cup	onion — minced
1	green pepper — diced
1	red pepper — diced

Sprinkle bacon and cheese over bottom of pie crust.

Beat eggs. Add all other ingredients and mix well.

Pour egg mixture over bacon and cheese.

Bake for 5 minutes at 400°. Reduce heat to 350° and bake 30 to 35 minutes longer or until set.

Sausage-filled Crepes

Servings: 8 • Preheat to 350°...

ook sausage and onion in a skillet over medium heat, stirring until sausage crumbles and is no longer pink.

Drain, then return the sausage to the skillet and add one cup cheddar cheese, cream cheese and marjoram, stirring until cheese melts.

Spoon 3 tablespoons of the filling down the center of each crepe. Roll the crepes up (not too tight) and place seam side down in a lightly greased baking dish.

Mix the sour cream and butter together and spoon over top of the crepes.

Bake uncovered until cheese has melted—approximately 10 minutes.

Garnish with remaining cheddar cheese and parsley.

Amt Measure	Ingredient — Preparation Method
1 pound	ground pork sausage
1 small	onion — diced
2 cups	cheddar cheese — shredded
3 ounces	cream cheese
1/2 teaspoon	marjoram
1/2 cup	sour cream
1/4 cup	butter — softened
1/4 cup	parsley — chopped
6	crepes

Salads

I . . . Thank you so much for providing everything necessary for such a nice evening — comfort, beauty, wonderful food, great hospitality, meeting new people — and just your special kindness. . . .

Broccoli and Cauliflower Marinated Salad

Servings: 12

Amt Measure	Ingredient — Preparation Method
2 heads	*broccoli — cut into flowerets*
1 head	*cauliflower — cut into flowerets*
1 cup	*mayonnaise*
1/2 cup	*sugar*
1/4 cup	*dill — chopped*

Mix broccoli and cauliflower in bowl.

Combine the mayonnaise, sugar and dill. Toss with vegetables.

Refrigerate overnight.

To Serve:
Line salad plates with lettuce leave.
Spoon broccoli and cauliflower mixture on lettuce.
Garnish with cherry tomatoes.
This is also a good salad for buffet dinners.

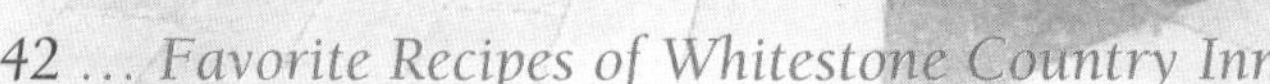

Caesar Salad

Servings:12

Break lettuce into small pieces. AT SERVING TIME, mix Caesar Salad Dressing and lettuce in large bowl until lettuce is coated.

Place on twelve salad plates. Sprinkle with Parmesan cheese and place four croutons on sides of plates.

Amt Measure	Ingredient — Preparation Method
2 heads	*romaine lettuce — chopped*
1/4 cup	*Parmesan cheese — grated*
48 1-inch	*croutons*

NOTES:

May serve with anchovies.

Caesar Dressing in on page 51.

Cauliflower Salad

Servings: 8

Amt Measure	Ingredient — Preparation Method
1 cup	*oil*
1/2 cup	*apple cider vinegar*
2 teaspoons	*sugar*
1 teaspoon	*salt*
1/2 teaspoon	*paprika*
1 head	*cauliflower flowerets*
1/2	*onion — sliced into rings*
1/3 cup	*stuffed green olives — sliced*
1/3 cup	*blue cheese — crumbled*
1 head	*leaf lettuce — shredded*

In a mixing bowl, combine the oil, vinegar, sugar, salt and paprika. Mix well.

Combine cauliflower, onion and olives in a large bowl and pour liquid mixture over vegetables.

Cover and refrigerate for 8 hours. Before serving add the cheese and lettuce.

Frozen Fruit Salad

Servings: 8

Mix together all the ingredients except the yogurt.
Put in shallow pan and freeze.
Cut in squares to serve.
Top with yogurt.

Amt Measure	Ingredient — Preparation Method
32 ounces	canned peaches — drained and chopped
21 ounces	crushed pineapple — drained
8 ounces	mandarin oranges — drained
6	bananas — finely chopped
12 ounces	concentrated orange juice — thawed
	peach or pineapple yogurt

NOTES:

This is also a good breakfast appetizer or dessert for winter when fresh fruits are scarce. Fresh strawberries and blueberries can be added in season.

Greek Salad

Servings: 6

Amt Measure	Ingredient — Preparation Method
1 medium	head romaine lettuce
1 stalk	celery — chopped
2	green onions — chopped
1	small cucumber — sliced
1	green pepper — julienned
2	tomatoes — wedged
12	Kalamata olives
1/2 pound	feta cheese — crumbled

Break lettuce into small pieces. Place in a salad bowl with celery, onions, cucumber, green pepper and tomatoes.

Toss with the Greek dressing on page 55.

Garnish the top with Kalamata olives and feta cheese.

Marinated Vegetable Salad

Servings: 12

Put green beans, olives, mushrooms and artichokes in a large bowl.

Add celery and onion, then mix well. In a jar, mix remaining ingredients. Pour over vegetables.

Cover and refrigerate overnight.

Serve over lettuce leaves.

NOTE:

Use tomato wedges or slices for garnish.

Amt Measure	Ingredient — Preparation Method
16 ounces	canned cut green beans — drained
16 ounces	pitted ripe olives — drained
16 ounces	mushroom stems and pieces — drained
16 ounces	artichoke hearts — drained and diced
1 1/2 cups	celery — chopped
1 medium	onion — sliced
1/4 cup	tarragon vinegar
1 1/2 teaspoons	Accent™ seasoning mix
1/4 teaspoon	salt
1/2 cup	olive oil
1/2 cup	Italian salad dressing

Spinach Salads

Servings: 6

Amt Measure	Ingredient — Preparation Method
2 quarts	*baby spinach leaves*

Citrus Spinach Salad:

2 cups	*grapefruit sections*
2 cups	*orange sections*
1/2 cup	*cottage cheese*
	French (page 54), ranch or raspberry vinegarette (page 60) dressing

Spinach Fruit Salad:

2 cups	*apples — sliced*
2 cups	*strawberries — sliced*
1 cup	*blueberries*
1 cup	*pineapple chunks — drained*
1/2 cup	*walnut halves*
	poppy seed dressing (page 59)

Apple Spinach Salad:

2	*Granny Smith apples — chopped*
1/2 cup	*salted cashews*
1/2 cup	*golden raisins*
1/4 cup	*sugar*
1 cup	*oil*
2 tablespoons	*balsamic vinegar*
1/4 teaspoon	*celery salt*

Citrus Spinach Salad:

Place spinach on salad plates and arrange grapefruit and orange segments over spinach. Place one teaspoon of cottage cheese in center and drizzle dressing over salad.

Spinach Fruit Salad:

Arrange spinach on salad plates. Alternate the fruit on the spinach and sprinkle walnut halves on top. Drizzle with poppy seed dressing.

Apple Spinach Salad:

Combine spinach, apples, cashews and raisins. Whisk together sugar, oil, vinegar and celery salt. Blend well. Pour mixture over salad. Toss gently and serve immediately.

Sauces & Salad Dressings

the gift of life —
the luxury and comfort —
beautiful scenery
and singing of birds
the wonder of it all —
what kind of place is
being prepared for us
in Heaven?

Apple & Raisin Sauce

Servings: 8

Amt Measure	Ingredient — Preparation Method
4 cups	apple juice
1 teaspoon	cinnamon
1/2 teaspoon	ground nutmeg
1/2 teaspoon	ground cloves
1/4 cup	raisins
1 tablespoon	cornstarch

In a medium saucepan, combine all ingredients and simmer for 20 minutes.

Thicken with some cornstarch dissolved in water to the desired consistency.

Serving Ideas: Serve over pork, French toast or pancakes.

Caesar Dressing

Servings: 12

Combine all ingredients and mix well.

Place in a container and refrigerate until cool.

Serve over Caesar Salad.

NOTE: Serve over Caesar Salad on page 43.

Amt Measure	Ingredient — Preparation Method
2 cups	mayonnaise
3 cloves	garlic — minced
1 tablespoon	worcestershire sauce
1 tablespoon	lemon juice
1/2 cup	oil
3 tablespoons	Parmesan cheese — grated
1 tablespoon	black pepper

Cherry-Walnut Vinaigrette

Servings: 12

Amt Measure	Ingredient — Preparation Method
1/8 cup	dried tart cherries
1/2 small	shallot
1 clove	garlic — peeled
1/3 cup	fruit-flavored vinegar
1/4 cup	orange juice
1 1/2 tablespoons	honey
3/4 cup	walnut oil
	salt and pepper to taste

Chop cherries, shallot and garlic in a food processor; pulse until finely chopped.

Add vinegar, orange juice and honey; puree.

With food processor on, slowly add walnut oil; mix well. Season with salt and pepper to taste.

NOTE:
Use dried tart cherries for garnish.

Citrus Vinaigrette

Servings: 8

In a food processor, combine all the ingredients except for the olive oil.

Blend well with the food processor running. Slowly pour the olive oil into the mixture. Pour this very slowly so that the ingredients incorporate.

Amt Measure	Ingredient — Preparation Method
3 tablespoons	fresh orange juice
1 tablespoon	lemon juice
1 teaspoon	lime juice
1 tablespoon	Dijon mustard
2 tablespoons	sweet basil leaves
	salt to taste
1/3 cup	olive oil

Cocktail Sauce

Servings: 8

Amt Measure	Ingredient — Preparation Method
3/4 cup	chili sauce
2 tablespoons	lemon juice
1 tablespoon	horseradish
2 teaspoons	Worcestershire sauce
	hot sauce to taste
	salt and pepper

In a mixing bowl, combine the chili sauce, lemon juice, horseradish and Worcestershire sauce. Mix well.

Add hot sauce to taste.

Salt and pepper to taste if needed.

NOTE:

Serve with your favorite shrimp dish.

You may add more horseradish if desired.

French Dressing

Servings: 8

Amt Measure	Ingredient — Preparation Method
2 teaspoons	salt
2 teaspoons	black pepper
1 teaspoon	chili powder
1 1/2 teaspoons	dry mustard
1 cup	sugar
1 cup	salad oil
1 cup	white vinegar
1/2 cup	onion — diced
13-ounce	can of tomato soup
	garlic powder to taste

Mix well. Refrigerate.

NOTE:

Will keep in refrigerator for a week.

Fresh Berry Compote

Servings: 6

Place all the berries and sugar in heavy saucepan.
Cook over high heat until sugar is dissolved and juices are released from the berries.
Mix cornstarch with lemon and orange juice. Add to berry mixture.
Cook one minute.
Remove from heat.

Amt Measure	Ingredient — Preparation Method
2 cups	fresh strawberries
2 cups	blueberries
1 cup	raspberries
1 cup	sugar
1 teaspoon	cornstarch
1 ounce	lemon juice
1 ounce	orange juice

NOTES:

Serve hot over plain cake, French toast or waffles.

Serve cold over ice cream.

Greek Dressing

Servings: 6

Whisk together all ingredients.
Serve over Greek Salad on page 46.

Amt Measure	Ingredient — Preparation Method
2/3 cup	olive oil
1/3 cup	red wine vinegar
1/4 cup	water
1 teaspoon	salt
1/4 teaspoon	black pepper
1 clove	garlic — minced
1 teaspoon	oregano

Hollandaise Sauce

Servings: 8

Amt Measure	Ingredient — Preparation Method
4	egg yolks
4 teaspoons	water
3 teaspoons	lemon juice
1/2 pound	butter
	salt and pepper

In a double boiler, add the yolks, water and lemon juice. Whisk until a yellowish color has been established. (Do not allow the water in the double boiler to touch the upper bowl containing the egg mixture.)

Remove from heat.

Stir in the butter a little at a time until incorporated and smooth.

Season with salt and pepper to taste.

Serving Ideas:

Serve over green vegetables or fish. Sprinkle with brown sugar for a nice flavor.

NOTE: May add 1/8 teaspoon of hot sauce.

Honey Nut Vinaigrette

Servings: 8

Combine all ingredients and blend well.

NOTE:
Serve over a Spinach or Garden Salad.

Amt Measure	Ingredient — Preparation Method
1/4 cup	honey
1/4 cup	oil
1 tablespoon	white vinegar
1/4 teaspoon	dry mustard
1/8 teaspoon	cinnamon
1/8 teaspoon	nutmeg
1/4 cup	chopped nuts

Lemon-Dill Vinaigrette

Servings: 8

Whisk all ingredients together. Refrigerate.

NOTE:
Serve over Garden Salad.

Amt Measure	Ingredient — Preparation Method
1/4 cup	lemon juice
1 teaspoon	dill weed
1 teaspoon	garlic salt
1/2 cup	olive oil
1 cup	mayonnaise

Peach Sauce

Servings: 8

Amt Measure	Ingredient — Preparation Method
1/2 teaspoon	cornstarch
1/2 teaspoon	water
16 ounces	canned peaches (juice packed) — drained
2 tablespoons	brown sugar
2 teaspoons	apple cider vinegar
1 teaspoon	cream sherry
1 teaspoon	Puerto Rican rum
1/4 teaspoon	ground cinnamon
1/4 teaspoon	ground nutmeg
1/4 teaspoon	ground cloves

In a saucepan, add cornstarch and water and stir until the cornstarch is dissolved.

Then add remaining ingredients and simmer for 10 to 12 minutes, stirring occasionally.

Sauce will thicken as it cooks.

Serving Idea:
Serve this sauce over the spicy pork chop recipe on page 88.

Poppy Seed Dressing

Servings: 8

In a blender or a food processor, combine sugar, onion salt, dry mustard and vinegar. Mix until well blended.

Gradually add oil. Beat for five minutes or until thick. Add poppy seeds.

Option: Add 1/2 cup blueberries after dressing is mixed. This would be called Blueberry Poppy Seed Dressing.

Amt Measure	Ingredient — Preparation Method
3/4 cup	sugar
1 1/2 teaspoons	onion salt
1 teaspoon	dry mustard
1/3 cup	white vinegar
1 cup	vegetable oil
1 tablespoon	poppy seeds

NOTE:
Serve over fruit and/or vegetable salads.

Raspberry Vinaigrette

Servings:12

Amt Measure	Ingredient — Preparation Method
2 cups	*vegetable oil*
2 cups	*raspberry puree*
1/2 cup	*balsamic vinegar*

Mix well.
Pour over salad just before serving.

Serving Ideas:
Garnish with a few fresh raspberries.

Soups

A Brief History

Soup is one of humanity's earliest culinary achievements. Although its exact beginnings are unknown, we know that primitive people fashioned fireproof vessels and began to cook meats, grains or vegetables in liquids. Since antiquity, soup has held an important place in the cuisine of every culture and its ingredients and preparation reflects the customs and economics of the times.

Earliest evidence indicates that in the Far East, by 8000 to 7000BC, cultivated grains were boiled in pottery vessels. The Bible tells how Esau sold his birthright to Jacob for a "pottage", a type of thick lentil soup.

The earliest cookbook in existence, written by Apices in first century Rome, offers recipes for barley soup and for a sweet liquid concoction of apricots, honey, wine, vinegar, peppermint and liquamen, a substance made from salted whole fish. This soup was available commercially in trade marked pots as early as 400BC.

By the 14th century, soup became more refined. In 1375, Gallium Lirel included recipes in his delicately phrased book, *Le Viandier*, for simple clear soups of ginger and garlic. He also included recipes for "garbure", a rich vegetable soup thickened with bread, as well as a "German Broth" made of wine, bacon, onions, almonds, cinnamon, ginger, cloves and saffron.

Scholars don't agree on the origin of the word "soup" but by the Middle Ages it had entered every European language in some form. Webster's *New World Dictionary* traces the English word "soup" back to the Medieval and Old English root words "soupen" and "supan", which means to sup or drink. The work "sup" also relates to the early Latin, French and German root word "suppa" which meant, "to eat the evening meal", hence our modern word "supper".

Georges Escoffier, who dominated the world of cuisine in the late 19th and early 20th Century, believed that soup and the stocks that made them were of utmost importance in modern cuisine.

In his world famous *Le Guide Culinaire*, Escoffier states "Stock is everything in cooking. If one's stock is good what remains of the work is easy."

While it was common in Escoffier's time for chefs to spend up to eight hours making a batch of soup stock, it's interesting to note that more than two-thirds of today's food service operations make their stocks for scratch soups using various kinds of soup bases.

Here at Whitestone Country Inn, we believe that the essential role of soup has changed little over 5000 years. Good soup is still the ultimate food for stimulating our appetites, nourishing our bodies and sustaining our spirits!   . . . *Chef Dodd Orton, Whitestone Country Inn*

Beef Barley Soup

Servings: 8

Amt Measure	Ingredient — Preparation Method
2 pounds	beef short ribs with bones
5 cups	water
14 1/2 ounces	canned diced tomatoes — undrained
1 medium	onion — chopped
1 teaspoon	salt
1/8 teaspoon	black pepper
2 cups	carrots — sliced
1 cup	celery — sliced
1 cup	cabbage — chopped
2/3 cup	quick-cooking pearl barley
1/4 cup	fresh parsley — chopped

In a kettle, combine ribs, water, tomatoes, onion, salt and pepper; bring to a boil over medium heat.

Reduce heat; cover and simmer for one to two hours or until the meat is tender.

Remove ribs and let cool; skim fat.

Remove meat from bones and cut into bite size pieces; return meat to broth.

Add carrots, celery and cabbage. Bring to a boil, reduce heat; cover and simmer for 15 minutes.

Add barley; return to a boil.

Reduce heat; cover and cook for 10 to 15 minutes or until barley and vegetables are tender.

Stir in the parsley.

Chilled Dill Summer Soup

Servings: 15

Sauté leeks in hot oil until tender. Add zucchini and broth.

Bring to a boil; cover and reduce heat. Simmer 8 to 10 minutes until zucchini is tender. Remove from heat; cool slightly.

Process mixture in a blender until smooth. Stir in half-and-half, sour cream, salt and chopped dill.

Chill at least 3 hours. Serve in small soup cups.

Amt Measure	Ingredient — Preparation Method
2 small	leeks — sliced
2 tablespoons	vegetable oil
1 1/2 pounds	zucchini or yellow squash — sliced
3 cups	chicken broth
1 cup	half and half
8 ounces	sour cream
1/2 teaspoon	salt
1/3 cup	fresh dill — chopped

NOTE:
Garnish with sprigs of fresh dill.

Chilled Mixed Fruit Soup

Servings: 8

Amt Measure	Ingredient — Preparation Method
1 cup	cranberry cocktail juice
1/2 cup	orange juice
1/4 teaspoon	vanilla extract
1 cup	apple juice
1/2 cup	pineapple juice
1/2 cup	strawberries
1 cup	peaches — chopped
1/2 cup	bananas — chopped
1/2 cup	peaches — sliced
1/2 cup	melon balls
1/2 cup	seedless grapes
1/2 cup	pineapple chunks in juice

In a food processor, puree first eight ingredients. Keep chilled.

When ready to serve, add remaining fruit to mixture.

Serve in fruit bowls with mint leaves as a garnish.

Cream of Broccoli Soup

Servings: 8

In a heavy stock pot, melt butter and add flour until roux forms.

Remove from heat and stir in water, chicken base, broccoli, salt, nutmeg and red pepper.

Heat to boiling over medium high heat.

Reduce heat and boil for 7 to 8 minutes until broccoli is tender. Remove from heat.

Add cream while stirring constantly. Heat to simmer.

Amt Measure	Ingredient — Preparation Method
3 sticks	butter
1 1/2 cups	all-purpose flour
1 gallon	hot water
4 1/2 ounces	chicken base
2 1/2 pounds	broccoli — frozen and chopped
1 teaspoon	salt
1/4 teaspoon	nutmeg
1/4 teaspoon	cayenne-red pepper
1 quart	heavy cream

NOTE:
Serve hot. Garnish with grated cheddar cheese.

Cream of Chicken Florentine Soup

Servings: 16

Amt Measure	Ingredient — Preparation Method
2 sticks	butter
1 cup	all-purpose flour
3 1/2 quarts	hot water
1/2 cup	chicken base
1 1/2 cup	chicken — cooked and cubed
1/3 cup	pimiento — chopped
2/3 cup	spinach — chopped
1/4 teaspoon	nutmeg
2 cups	half and half

Cook butter and flour until blended.

Add the next 6 ingredients and simmer.

Finish by adding half & half.

Cream together.

Cream of Mushroom Soup

Servings: 4

In a 4-quart stock pot, heat heavy cream, mushrooms and mushroom base until boiling.

Reduce heat and simmer 8 to 10 minutes until mushrooms are cooked.

Mix flour and butter to form a paste. Add to soup, stirring constantly.

Stir in white wine.

Salt and pepper to taste.

Amt Measure	Ingredient — Preparation Method
2 quarts	heavy cream
1 quart	fresh mushrooms — sliced
3 ounces	mushroom base
1 stick	unsalted butter—melted
1/2 cup	all-purpose flour
1 cup	dry white wine
	salt and pepper

NOTE:
Serve hot.

Cream of Peach Soup

Servings: 10

Amt Measure	Ingredient — Preparation Method
2 pounds	ripe peaches
1/4 cup	sugar
1 cup	water
1 cup	whipping cream
1/2 cup	white wine
1	lemon rind — grated

Remove skins from peaches by dipping into boiling water for one minute.

Immediately plunge peaches into ice water to stop the cooking process.

Drain and slip the skins off.

Cut peaches into quarters.

Combine sugar and water in a large saucepan and bring to a boil over medium heat.

Reduce heat; add peaches; cover and simmer 5 minutes. Cool.

In batches, process mixture in a blender until smooth.

Combine peach mixture, whipping cream, wine and lemon rind. Chill.

Serve in small soup cups.

NOTES:
Garnish with fresh sprigs of mint and fresh strawberries.

French Onion Soup

Servings: 4

In a large soup pot over high heat, combine beef and chicken stock, peppercorns and half of thc onion.

Bring to boil. Reduce to low and simmer.

Melt butter in a large skillet over medium-high heat.

Add remaining onions and sauté until soft and translucent.

Drain off any grease and add onions to soup pot mixture.

Continue to simmer soup over low heat for two hours.

Add sherry and simmer 1/2 hour or until onions are tender.

Divide equally between four bowls.

Sprinkle with croutons; cover bowl with a slice of Swiss cheese and top with grated Parmesan cheese.

Place under a pre-heated broiler and cook until cheese is melted, bubbly and golden brown.

Serve at once.

Amt Measure	Ingredient — Preparation Method
6 cups	beef stock
2 cups	chicken stock
3	peppercorns — whole
1 pound	yellow onions — peeled and sliced thin
2 tablespoons	butter
1/8 cup	dry sherry
1 cup	croutons
4 slices	Swiss cheese
	Parmesan cheese — grated

Tomato Basil Soup

Servings:12

Combine all ingredients except cream.

Heat to boiling over medium heat.

Reduce heat, add cream.

Stir constantly. Cook approximately 20 minutes.

NOTE:
Garnish with fresh basil and shredded Parmesan cheese.

Amt Measure	Ingredient — Preparation Method
6 lbs-9-ounce	peeled pear tomatoes — canned, pureed
1/4 cup	dried basil
1/8 cup	granulated garlic
1/4 cup	Parmesan cheese — grated
1 tablespoon	salt
1/4 cup	sugar
1/2 tablespoon	black pepper
3/4 cup	heavy cream

Tomato Bisque

Servings: 16

Amt Measure	Ingredient — Preparation Method
1 1/2 sticks	butter — melted
3/4 cup	all-purpose flour
3 1/2 quarts	hot water
3 ounces	chicken base
12 ounces	tomato paste
14 ounces	tomatoes — canned, diced
1/2 cup	sugar
2 teaspoons	salt
1 cup	heavy cream

In heavy stock pot, melt butter then add flour. Stir until bubbly.

Remove from heat and stir in water, chicken base, tomato paste, tomatoes, sugar and salt. Heat to boiling.

Boil and stir one or two minutes.

Remove from heat then stir in cream and reheat to simmer.

Serve hot.

Vermont Cheese Soup

Servings:16

In a heavy pot over medium heat, melt butter. Stir in onions, celery, carrots and green peppers. Sauté 5 to 6 minutes.

Add flour. Stir constantly over heat until well blended.

Add the hot water and chicken base. Simmer for about 7 minutes.

Add cheese and half and half and cook until cheese melts. Serve hot.

Amt Measure	Ingredient — Preparation Method
2 sticks	butter
3/4 cup	onions — diced
3/4 cup	celery — diced
3/4 cup	carrots — diced
1/2 cup	grecn pcppers — diced
1 cup	all-purpose flour
3 quarts	hot water
3 ounces	chicken base
4 ounces	American cheese — diced
8 ounces	Cheddar cheese
2 cups	half and half

NOTE:
Garnish with thin strips of green pepper.

Whitestone Minestrone Soup

Servings:16

Amt Measure	Ingredient — Preparation Method
32 ounces	bean soup mix
8 cups	warm water
2 tablespoons	butter
8 stalks	celery — chopped
2 cups	onion — chopped
3 cloves	garlic — crushed
12	carrots — peeled & sliced thin
2 teaspoons	marjoram
4	bay leaves
2 teaspoons	basil
2 teaspoons	salt
1 teaspoon	black pepper
64-ounces	canned crushed tomatoes
3 pounds	smoked ham — cubed

Pick through soup mix discarding little stones, etc. from the beans. Wash beans. Pour eight cups warm water in a kettle. Add beans and let soak overnight. Drain and rinse beans.

Sauté celery, onion and garlic in butter.

Combine all the ingredients. Bring to a boil and simmer until beans are tender (1 to 2 hours).

If the soup is too thick, add some water until desired consistency is established.

Meats

. . . We've been so-o-o blessed with a wonderful "experience," the "Whitestone Experience!" We enjoyed every minute!

. . .

Thank you for making your dream a reality for all who come through this place looking for a refuge!

Apple Pork

Servings: 8 • Preheat to 350°...

Amt Measure	Ingredient — Preparation Method
5 pounds	*pork loin roast — boneless*
1 quart	*apple cider*
1 tablespoon	*cinnamon*
1/2 tablespoon	*ground nutmeg*
1/2 tablespoon	*ground cloves*
	chopped nuts for garnish

Place the roast in a roasting pan and pour the apple cider over the loin.

Sprinkle seasonings over roast and cover with foil.

Bake for one hour; remove the foil and bake until the fat turns a golden brown.

Serve the sliced pork with apple raisin sauce on page 50 and garnish with chopped nuts.

NOTES:

May add 4 apples (cut in half) while baking the pork. Serve with the roast.

Braised Meatballs in Red Wine Gravy

Servings: 8 • Preheat to 350°...

Combine bread and milk in medium bowl to submerge. Let stand until milk is absorbed about 10 minutes. Squeeze out milk and discard. Place bread (milk-soaked) in large bowl.

Add beef, eggs, onion, 1/2 cup parsley, salt, pepper and dried summer savory. Mix well.

Transfer to processor. Process until well blended and mixture looks pasty. Form into 1 3/4" meatballs. Divide meatballs into two 9"x13" baking dishes.

Bake 30 minutes. Set aside. Cool. Dust meatballs with flour and shake off excess.

Melt butter and oil in large skillet over medium high heat working in batches. Add meatballs and sauté until brown on all sides about 3 minutes. Return all meatballs to skillet.

Whisk wine, tomato paste and remaining parsley until blended. Add wine mixture to meatballs and bring to a boil. Boil until it starts to thicken stirring constantly.

Amt Measure	Ingredient — Preparation Method
6 ounces	French bread
1 cup	milk
1 3/4 pounds	ground beef (7-15% fat)
2 large	eggs
1 medium	onion — chopped fine
1/2 cup + 1 tbsp	parsley
2 teaspoons	salt
1 teaspoon	ground black pepper
1 teaspoon	summer savory
	all-purpose flour for dusting meatballs
2 tablespoons	butter
1 1/2 teaspoons	olive oil
2 cups	dry port red wine
1/4 cup	tomato paste
3 cups	beef broth (use beef base)

NOTE:
Serve 3 meatballs per person.

Add broth. Reduce heat and simmer until flavors blend and gravy thickens.

Chicken Marsala

Servings: 4

Amt Measure	Ingredient — Preparation Method
4	*chicken breasts — boneless, skinless*
1 tablespoon	*butter*
1 1/2 cups	*fresh mushrooms — sliced*
2 tablespoons	*green onions — sliced*
2 cups	*Marsala wine*
2 cloves	*garlic — minced*
	salt to taste

Lightly pound chicken breasts to about 1/4" thick.

Melt butter in a large skillet over medium heat and cook the chicken breast in the skillet until no pink remains. Remove chicken but keep warm.

Add the mushrooms to the skillet and sauté until soft.

Add garlic and sauté for two minutes.

Pour Marsala wine into skillet and let mixture cook until done. This will take about 8 to 10 minutes.

Salt to taste.

Place one chicken breast on a plate and spoon sauce over the chicken.

NOTE:
The chicken can be replaced by using veal or pork.

Crab Au Gratin

Servings: 6 • Preheat to 350°...

Sauté the onion, celery and carrots in butter until soft.

Add flour to mixture and blend.

Add milk and blend.

Remove from heat; gently fold in the egg yolks, crabmeat, salt and pepper.

Put in casserole dish and cover with cheese.

Bake for 15 to 20 minutes or until cheese has melted.

Amt Measure	Ingredient — Preparation Method
1 large	onion — diced
3 stalks	celery — diced
1 large	carrot — peeled & diced
1/2 pound	butter
4 tablespoons	all-purpose flour
1 large can	evaporated milk
2	egg yolks — slightly beaten
1 pound	fresh white crab meat
	salt and pepper to taste
10 ounces	cheddar cheese — shredded

NOTE:

Shrimp can be substituted in place of crab meat.

Flank Steak Pinwheels

Servings: 6

Amt Measure	Ingredient — Preparation Method
8 slices	bacon
2 pounds	flank steak
	kosher salt
	black pepper
2 cloves	garlic bulbs — minced
	Italian seasoning
10 ounces	frozen, chopped spinach — thawed and drained
1/4 cup	Parmesan cheese — grated

In a large skillet, cook bacon until just done but not crisp; remove and drain.

Score the flank steak with shallow cuts at one-inch intervals diagonally across steak in a diamond pattern. Repeat procedure on other side of steak.

Pound the steak into a 12"x8" rectangle working from the center of the steak to the outer edges.

Season with salt, pepper, garlic and Italian seasonings.

Place bacon lengthwise on steak.

Spread the spinach over the bacon.

Cover with Parmesan cheese.

Roll steak from short end and secure it with toothpicks at one-inch intervals.

Cut between toothpicks into 8 one-inch slices.

Place cut side down on a broiler pan.

Broil on both sides until desired doneness is established. Remove picks and serve.

NOTES:

You can also grill these steaks on skewers.

These are good served with a mushroom or demi-glaze sauce.

Garlic Buttered Shrimp

Servings: 4

In a sauté pan, heat the butter over medium high heat.

Add the shrimp and garlic, stirring occasionally for three minutes or until the shrimp has become pink in color throughout.

Stir in remaining ingredients and cook for three more minutes covered.

Amt Measure	Ingredient — Preparation Method
2 tablespoons	butter
1 pound	shrimp (21-25) — peeled and deveined
3 cloves	garlic — minced
2 tablespoons	fresh parsley — chopped
2 tablespoons	dry white wine
1 tablespoon	Parmesan cheese — grated
	salt and pepper to taste
2 medium	lemons — juice only

NOTES:

These can be served on skewers for an appetizer or as an accompaniment with beef.

Grilled Honey Mustard Chicken

Servings: 6

Amt Measure	Ingredient — Preparation Method
1/4 cup	Dijon mustard
3 tablespoons	honey
2 tablespoons	butter — melted
1 tablespoon	lemon juice
1 clove	garlic bulbs — minced
6	chicken breasts
	toasted almonds for garnish

In a mixing bowl, combine mustard, honey, butter, lemon juice and garlic.

Grill chicken for 10 to 15 minutes, turning occasionally and brushing with the mustard mixture frequently.

Garnish with toasted almonds.

Hot and Sour Chicken Kabobs

Servings: 4

Melt the butter; add oil, juice, garlic and hot sauce.

Simmer to blend flavors—about 30 minutes.

Pour marinade over chicken cubes; refrigerate for three hours.

Thread chicken cubes on skewers.

Broil, bake or grill until done.

Amt Measure	Ingredient — Preparation Method
1/4 cup	butter
1/4 cup	peanut oil
4 tablespoons	lime juice
4 cloves	garlic — minced
2 tablespoons	hot sauce
1 1/2 pounds	chicken tenders — cubed 3/4" thick

NOTE:

Excellent served with wild rice or rice pilaf.

Key Lime Chicken

Servings: 6 • Preheat to 350°...

Amt Measure	Ingredient — Preparation Method
6 ounces	boneless, skinless chicken breasts
1/2 cup	lime juice
3 cloves	garlic — minced
3 teaspoons	ground ginger
1 cup	all-purpose flour
1 teaspoon	garlic powder
1 teaspoon	salt
1 teaspoon	black pepper
	peanut oil for frying
1 cup	chicken stock
	brown sugar

Trim fat from chicken and pound to slightly flatten. Marinate in bowl with lime juice, garlic, and 2 teaspoons ground ginger for 30 minutes.

Drain the marinade from chicken.

Mix flour, 1 teaspoon ground ginger, garlic powder, salt and pepper in a bowl.

Lightly dredge the chicken breasts through the flour covering both sides. Heat peanut oil in a sauté pan. Fry the chicken until browned on both sides. (Do not overcook.)

Place the fried chicken in a sprayed baking dish. Add the chicken stock. Sprinkle brown sugar on the chicken breasts.

Bake 20 to 30 minutes.

The brown sugar will caramelize and become a crunchy topping.

NOTE:

Garnish with a lime twist and a mint leaf.

Poached Salmon Fillets

Servings: 2

In a medium saucepan, combine the water, wine and pickling spice.

Allow the mixture to boil for one hour to season the water.

When ready to cook the fish, bring the water to a simmer and add the fish.

Cook the fish until pale pink.

Garnish with lemon slice.

Amt Measure	Ingredient — Preparation Method
1 quart	water
1/2 cup	white wine
2 tablespoons	pickling spice
2	salmon fillets
2	lemon slices for garnish

Pork Boudreaux

Serving Size: 1

Amt Measure	Ingredient — Preparation Method
Demi Glacé:	
1 tablespoon	butter — melted
1 tablespoon	flour
2 cups	veal or beef stock
Meat:	
6 ounces	pork tenderloin — cut into medallions
1 ounce	butter
	flour for dredging meat
1 pinch	Cajun Spice
1/2 ounce	brandy
	green, red & yellow peppers — cut into strips
1/2 cup	demi-glacé
1/2 cup	pork stock

Make roux with butter and flour. Let it get dark. Add stock and cook until it thickens.

First, pound pork medallions until they are 3 to 4 inches in diameter. Heat butter in sauté pan.

Dredge pork in flour and shake off excess. Place pork in pan; add spice and cook for 3 to 4 minutes. Turn and cook 1 to 2 minutes.

Deglaze pan with brandy. Add peppers and cook one minute. Add pork, pork stock and demi-glacé. Simmer 3 to 4 minutes.

Pork Piccata

Servings: 8

Thinly slice the pork and pound lightly. Combine the flour, salt and pepper and dredge pork through flour mixture.

In a skillet, heat the olive oil and cook pork on both sides until browned. (DO NOT OVERCOOK).

Remove from pan and keep pork warm.

For the sauce, pour off the oil in skillet. Add garlic and mushrooms.

Sauté for two minutes stirring often.

Add wine and stock. Bring to a boil. Reduce mixture to 1/2 cup; this takes about 8 to 10 minutes.

Stir in capers, lemon zest and juice. Return to a boil. Slowly stir in butter and parsley and cook until sauce is thick and creamy.

To serve, dip the pork into the sauce and arrange on a plate in a fan-like pattern.

Spoon some sauce over the plated pork.

Amt Measure	Ingredient — Preparation Method
1 1/2 pounds	pork tenderloin
1 cup	all-purpose flour
1 teaspoon	salt
1 teaspoon	black pepper
1/2 cup	olive oil
1 large	garlic clove — minced
1/2 pound	fresh mushrooms — sliced
1/2 cup	dry white wine
1/2 cup	chicken stock
3 tablespoons	capers
1	lemon — zest and juice
2 tablespoons	butter
2 tablespoons	parsley — chopped

NOTE:

Substitute veal, turkey or chicken in place of the pork.

Spicy Pork Chops

Servings: 4

Amt Measure	Ingredient — Preparation Method
1 teaspoon	marjoram leaves
1 teaspoon	thyme leaves
2 cloves	garlic—minced
1/4 teaspoon	red pepper — ground
	hot sauce to taste
1 pound	boneless pork loin chops

Combine spices in a bowl and rub on both sides of chops.

You can bake, broil or grill these.

Pork is done when an internal temperature of 180° has been reached.

NOTE:

We serve these with the peach sauce recipe on page 58.

Sweet and Sour Pork Loin

Servings: 8

Combine all ingredients except the pork to make marinade. Mix well.

Put the pork loin in a plastic bag and pour the marinade into the bag.

Close bag and refrigerate overnight.

To cook, remove the pork from the bag (save the marinade for basting).

Place pork on a grill over very low heat. Close the hood of the grill.

Grill for 1 1/2 hours or until an internal temperature of 180° has been reached.

Brush the reserved marinade on the roast frequently during the last 45 minutes for cooking.

Let roast stand for 20 minutes before carving.

Amt Measure	Ingredient — Preparation Method
1 cup	brown sugar — packed
3/4 cup	teriyaki sauce
3/4 cup	red wine
3/4 cup	chili sauce
1 clove	garlic — minced
1/4 teaspoon	black pepper
1/8 teaspoon	kosher salt
5 pounds	boneless pork loin — fold in half and tie

Side Dishes

Today, I walked my little girl down the aisle. How fast they do grow!

It was she who chose this great place. Everyone at the Inn has been superb.

One cannot help feeling right at home here; ...

The serenity of this place is amazing. ...

It looks just like a picture postcard. ...

Corn Cakes

Servings: 8

Amt Measure	Ingredient — Preparation Method
4 slices	bacon — cut into 1/2 pieces
1 pound	frozen corn
1/4 cup	water
1/4 cup	pimientos
1/2 cup	green onions — sliced
1/4 cup	fresh parsley
1 tablespoon	lemon juice
1 teaspoon	salt
1 teaspoon	sugar
1/2 teaspoon	oregano
1/2 teaspoon	cumin
pinch	black pepper
1/2 cup	heavy cream
3 large	eggs — separated
1/2 cup	all-purpose flour
1/4 teaspoon	baking powder

Cook bacon, drain drippings and save.

Add corn and water to same skilled and cook until dry.

Mix bacon, pimiento and next eight ingredients into corn.

Add heavy cream and egg yolks; mix well.

Add flour and baking powder.

Beat egg whites; stir 1/4 into batter. Fold in remainder of egg whites.

Heat large griddle; add bacon fat.

Spoon batter 1/4 cup at a time onto a hot griddle.

Cook until golden brown about 2 minutes. Turn cake and brown.

NOTE:

May be served for breakfast or dinner.

Corn Pudding

Servings: 6 • Preheat to 350°...

With a wire whisk, mix corn and flour. Add remaining ingredients and mix well.

Pour into buttered two quart baking dish.

Bake for one hour or until set.

Amt Measure	Ingredient — Preparation Method
2 1/2 cups	creamed corn
5 tablespoons	all-purpose flour
1 teaspoon	sugar
1 teaspoon	salt
1/4 cup	butter — melted
3/4 cup	milk
3	eggs — beaten

NOTE:

Serve for breakfast or dinner.

Dried Cherry Butternut Squash Stuffing

Servings: 24

Amt Measure	Ingredient — Preparation Method
3/4 cup	pancetta — finely diced (may use Italian or smoked sausage)
3/4 cup	unsalted butter
1 1/2 cups	onion — diced
4 1/2 cups	butternut squash — diced
2 1/4 cups	dried tart cherries
1/4 cup	sage — chopped
3/4 cup	hazelnuts — toasted, skinned and finely ground
	breadcrumbs
3/4 cup	chicken broth
	salt and pepper

Sauté pancetta 5 to 7 minutes or until crisp. Remove pancetta to a large mixing bowl.

Add butter to the pancetta drippings. Sauté onion and squash 3 to 5 minutes or until semi-soft.

Add cherries and sage; continue cooking until squash is soft.

Combine squash mixture to pancetta.

Stir in hazelnuts and bread crumbs; mix thoroughly.

Add broth mixture a little at a time to obtain the right consistency. Add more bread crumbs if mixture is too wet; add more broth to add moisture.

Season with salt and pepper to taste.

NOTE:

Substitute dried cranberries in place of cherries.

Glazed Carrots with Dried Cherries

Servings: 6

Cook carrots, in boiling water 8 to 10 minutes, or until tender. Drain.

Heat cherries, syrup, butter, nutmeg, ginger and salt in saucepan.

Stir in carrots and heat until carrots are well glazed.

Amt Measure	Ingredient — Preparation Method
3/4 pound	baby carrots
1/2 cup	dried tart cherries
1/4 cup	maple syrup
2 tablespoons	butter or margarine
1/2 teaspoon	ground nutmeg
1/3 teaspoon	ground ginger
1/8 teaspoon	salt

Pineapple Casserole

Servings: 6 • Preheat to 350°...

Amt Measure	Ingredient — Preparation Method
20 ounces	canned pineapple chunks
1/2 cup	sugar
3 tablespoons	all-purpose flour
1 cup	grated cheese
1/4 cup	melted butter
1/2 cup	butter flavored snack cracker crumbs

Drain pineapple chunks reserving 3 tablespoons of juice. Combine sugar, flour and juice. Add cheese and pineapple.

Spoon into a 1 quart casserole dish. Combine butter and cracker crumbs and sprinkle over the pineapple mixture.

Bake for 25 minutes. Topping will be golden brown.

NOTES:

If you like more crispy topping, you can add more cracker crumbs.

This is a great side dish to serve with ham. Can be used for breakfast or dinner as side dish or an appetizer.

Scalloped Tomatoes

Servings: 6 • Preheat to 375°...

Sauté onion in butter and stir in bread cubes, salt and basil.

To assemble:
In a casserole dish, layer the tomato slices with liquid; sprinkle lightly with sugar and 1/4 of the bread cube mixture.

Repeat four times ending with bread cubes as the top layer.

Bake for 30 minutes or until hot and bubbly.

Amt Measure	Ingredient — Preparation Method
1/4 cup	butter
1 small	onion — chopped
2 cups	fresh bread — cubed
1 teaspoon	salt
1/4 teaspoon	sweet basil leaves
14 ounces	canned small tomatoes — sliced
1 teaspoon	sugar

NOTE:
We serve this as a side dish for breakfast, however, it could also be used for dinner.

Spiced Fruit

Servings: 8 • Preheat to 350°...

Amt Measure	Ingredient — Preparation Method
1 large	can peach halves — save the juice
1 large	can pears — drained
1 large	can apricots — drained
1 large	can pineapple chunks — drained
1 pint	fresh cherries
1/2 cup	brown sugar — packed
1 tablespoon	cinnamon
3 tablespoons	butter

Combine fruits and spread in baking dish.

In saucepan, combine brown sugar, cinnamon, butter and the juice of the peaches.

Simmer until the brown sugar has dissolved.

Pour mixture over the fruit and bake at 350° until bubbly.

NOTE:

Serve hot for breakfast or as a side dish for dinner.

Whitestone

Desserts & Pies

" . . . Be still and know that I am God."…
And, sometimes that is just what we need to do.
What a wonderful place to "be still" and experience
God's love and mercy.
… Our visit has been such a pleasure. You've truly helped make
this time "Golden!"…

Black Bottom Pie

Serving Size: 16

Amt Measure	Ingredient — Preparation Method
1 cup	*sugar*
3 tablespoons	*cornstarch*
8	*egg yolks*
4 cups	*half and half — scalded*
3 envelopes	*unflavored gelatin*
1/2 cup	*warm water*
3 squares	*chocolate — melted*
1 teaspoon	*vanilla*
2 9-inch	*chocolate crumb pie shells*

Custard Topping:

8	*egg whites*
1/2 teaspoon	*cream of tartar*
3/4 cup	*sugar*
3 tablespoons	*rum*
	whipped cream for garnishing
	chocolate curls for garnishing

In the top of a double boiler combine sugar, cornstarch, egg yolks and scalded half and half.

Cook over boiling water, stirring until thick enough to coat a spoon.

Soften gelatin in warm water and add to custard mixture. Divide custard mixture in half.

To one part add melted chocolate and vanilla. Pour into the 2 pie shells.

Chill until firm.

Top with custard topping.

Custard Topping:

Beat egg whites with cream of tartar.

Gradually add 3/4 cup sugar and beat until stiff. Add rum to remaining custard and fold in the egg whites.

Spread mixture over chocolate pies. Chill until firm. Garnish with whipped cream and chocolate curls.

Chocolate Chip Pie

Servings: 8 • Preheat to 325°...

Beat eggs until foamy.

Add flour, sugar and brown sugar. Blend until mixture becomes smooth.

Add margarine and stir in chocolate chips.

Pour mixture into the pie shell and bake for one hour. Check for doneness by using a toothpick.

Amt Measure	Ingredient — Preparation Method
2	eggs
1/2 cup	all-purpose flour
1/2 cup	sugar
1/2 cup	brown sugar
1/2 cup	margarine — melted
1 cup	chocolate chips
1 9-inch	pie shell — unbaked

Chocolate Coconut Cream Pie

Servings: 8

Amt Measure	Ingredient — Preparation Method
1 8-inch	pie crust
1/2 cup	nuts (pecans, walnuts, macadamias) — chopped
2/3 cup	sugar
1/3 cup	cornstarch
1/4 teaspoon	salt
3 cups	half and half
3	eggs — slightly beaten
1 tablespoon	butter
2 tablespoons	vanilla
1/2 cup	coconut — flaked
3 tablespoons	powdered cocoa
3 tablespoons	sugar
2 tablespoons	half and half
	whipped cream for garnish
	toasted coconut and chocolate curls for garnishing

Sprinkle chopped nuts over the bottom of pie crust. Bake pie crust. Set aside to cool.

In saucepan, stir together sugar, cornstarch, salt and 3 cups half and half.

Blend in eggs and cook over medium heat, stirring constantly until mixture boils. Continue stirring and boil for one minute. Remove from heat. Stir in butter and vanilla. Pour 1 1/2 cups of the cream filling into a small bowl. Add coconut. Pour coconut filling into baked pie crust.

Stir together cocoa, 3 tablespoons sugar and 2 tablespoons half and half. Blend in the remaining filling in saucepan.

Return to the heat. Heat just to the boiling point, stirring constantly. Remove from heat; cool slightly. Pour over coconut filling. Cover with plastic wrap and refrigerate until cold.

Before serving, garnish with whipped cream, toasted coconut and chocolate curls.

Chocolate Peanut Butter Pie

Servings: 8 • Preheat to 350°...

Amt Measure	Ingredient — Preparation Method
Crust:	
1 1/4 cups	pretzels — finely crushed
1/2 cup	sugar
1 stick	butter — melted
Pie Filling:	
6 mini	peanut butter cups — chopped
1 pint	whipping cream
1/2 cup	powdered sugar
1 cup	creamy peanut butter
8 ounces	cream cheese — softened
1 cup	powdered sugar
2 teaspoons	vanilla

Crust:

Combine pretzel crumbs, sugar and butter. Mix well and press Into a 9" pie pan.

Bake for 6 to 8 minutes. Remove and cool completely.

Pie Filling:

Spread peanut butter cups into cooled crust.

Whip cream until soft peaks form.

Add 1/2 cup powdered sugar and whip until peaks are stiff. Set aside.

In large bowl, cream peanut butter and cream cheese.

Add one cup powdered sugar and combine well.

Add vanilla and beat for one minute on high speed.

Fold whipped cream into cream cheese mixture until completely blended.

Spoon into pie shell.

Chill well before serving.

NOTE:

Garnish with peanuts and/or chocolate syrup.

Chocolate Swirl Cheesecake

Servings: 8 • Preheat to 350°...

Amt Measure	Ingredient — Preparation Method
4 squares	*sem-sweet chocolate*
16 ounces	*cream cheese — softened*
1/2 cup	*sugar — divided*
2	*eggs*
1/2 teaspoon	*vanilla*
1 9-inch	*graham cracker crust*
	whipped cream for garnish
	fresh strawberries for garnish

Melt chocolate.

Whisk 8 ounces of cream cheese, 1/4 cup sugar and one egg into the melted chocolate until well blended.

Pour into crust.

Whisk remaining cream cheese, sugar, egg and vanilla until well blended.

Spoon batter over the chocolate in the crust. Use a teaspoon to swirl batters together.

Bake for 40 minutes or until center is almost set.

Cool and refrigerate three hours or overnight.

NOTE:
Garnish with whipped cream and fresh strawberries.

Chocolate Truffle Torte

Servings:12 • Preheat to 350°...

Cake:

Melt the margarine and chocolate chips together until smooth. Cool for 10 minutes.

In a mixing bowl, beat the eggs, sugar, vanilla and salt for 4 minutes or until thick.

Blend in the chocolate mixture.

Stir in the flour and mix well.

Pour into a greased and floured 9-inch springform pan.

Bake for 25 to 30 minutes or until a toothpick inserted into the middle comes out clean.

Cool completely on a wire rack.

Glaze:

Combine the glaze ingredients in a small saucepan; cook and stir over low heat until melted and smooth. Cool slightly.

Run a knife around the edge of the springform pan to loosen, then remove cake to serving plate.

Spread glaze over the top and sides of the cake and allow to chill in a refrigerator for two hours.

Amt Measure	Ingredient — Preparation Method
Cake:	
1/2 cup	margarine
1 cup	chocolate chips
3	eggs
2/3 cup	sugar
1 teaspoon	vanilla
1/4 teaspoon	salt
2/3 cup	all-purpose flour
Glaze:	
1/4 cup	margarine
3/4 cup	chocolate chips
2 teaspoons	honey

NOTES:

We serve this with a raspberry sauce and garnish with whipped cream and fresh mint leaf.

Chocolate Brownies with Ganache

Servings: 12 • Preheat to 350°...

Amt Measure	Ingredient — Preparation Method
1/2 cup	all-purpose flour
1 1/2 teaspoons	cinnamon
1/8 teaspoon	salt
6 ounces	semi-sweet chocolate — chopped
3/4 cup	unsalted butter — cut in small pieces
4 large	eggs
1 cup	sugar
1 1/2 teaspoons	vanilla extract
1 cup	walnuts or pecans — chopped

Ganache:

6 ounces	semi-sweet chocolate — chopped
3 tablespoons	butter — room temperature
2 tablespoons	heavy cream

Mix first three ingredients in small bowl.

Combine chocolate and butter (room temperature) in top of double boiler until melted and smooth. Turn off heat. Let set over the boiling hot water.

Beat eggs and sugar in mixer until mixture thickens and forms ribbons. Beat in vanilla.

Add the flour mixture in two additions blending well after each addition.

Gradually add warm chocolate to egg mixture. Beat until combined.

Stir in nuts. Pour mixture into a well buttered, floured 8-inch square pan. Bake in center of oven for about 35 minutes until tester comes out with moist crumbs. Cool in pan.

Ganache:

Whisk all the ingredients in saucepan over medium heat until melted and smooth.

Pour evenly over pan of warm brownies. Let set until cool about 2 hours.

Cut into squares and serve.

Fresh Strawberry Shortcake

Servings: 8 • Preheat to 375°...

In saucepan, combine one pint of strawberries, 1/2 cup sugar and lemon juice.

Bring to a boil. Cook over moderately high heat for 10 minutes, stirring constantly. It should be thick and reduced to 1 1/2 cups.

Let cool completely. Add the rest of the strawberries and let stand for one hour.

Shortcake:

Sift the flour, 2 tablespoons sugar, baking powder and salt. Blend in butter with pastry blender.

Add lemon peel with finger tips until mixture resembles coarse meal. Stir in enough heavy cream to make a soft dough.

Form dough into ball. Roll or pat out 1/2" thick rounds (2 1/2 to 3" diameter).

Arrange on buttered baking sheet. Brush tops with milk and sprinkle with sugar.

Bake 15 to 20 minutes until puffed and golden.

Split biscuits with a fork and butter the bottom halves. Mound with berry mixture. Cover with top half of biscuit. Garnish with whipped cream and mint leaves.

Amt Measure	Ingredient — Preparation Method
3 pints	strawberries — halved and sliced
1/2 cup	sugar
1/4 cup	lemon juice
Shortcake:	
2 cups	all-purpose flour
2 tablespoons	sugar
1 tablespoon	baking powder
1/2 teaspoon	salt
2 tablespoons	butter, unsalted — cut into bits
1 1/2 teaspoons	lemon peel — minced
1 cup	heavy cream
	milk for brushing over biscuits
	sugar for sprinkling over biscuits
	butter — melted for spreading
	whipped cream for garnish
	mint leaves for garnish

Key Lime Pie

Servings: 8 • Preheat to 325°...

Amt Measure	Ingredient — Preparation Method
1 8-inch	pie crust — baked or graham cracker crust
3	eggs — separated
14 ounces	sweetened condensed milk (1 1/4 cup)
3/4 teaspoon	key lime peel — finely shredded
1/2 cup	water
1/3 cup	lime juice (8-10 key limes)
	several drops green food coloring (optional)
	whipped cream for garnishing
	lime twists for garnishing

Beat egg yolks with a rotary beater.

Gradually stir in sweetened condensed milk and lime peel.

Add water, lime juice and food coloring.

Mix well (mixture will thicken).

Spoon thickened filling into pie shell.

Bake for 30 minutes.

Chill 3 to 6 hours before serving.

Cover for longer storage.

NOTES:
Garnish with whipped cream and lime twist or make a meringue with the egg whites.

Lemon Chiffon Pie

Servings: 8

Place egg whites in large bowl of electric mixer. Let whites warm to room temperature.

Sprinkle gelatin over 1/4 cup cold water to soften. Set aside.

Place yolks in a double boiler. With wooden spoon, beat egg yolks slightly. Stir in lemon juice, 1/2 cup sugar and the salt. Cook until mixture thickens and forms coating on spoon.

Add gelatin. Stir to dissolve. Add lemon peel and 2 drops of yellow food coloring. Remove from heat.

Pour into bowl and set in ice cubes to chill until thick.

Beat whites until soft peaks form. Beat in 1/2 cup sugar adding only 2 tablespoons at a time. Beat well after each addition. Beat until stiff peaks form. Gently fold egg yolks mixture and gelatin into egg whites.

Beat 1/2 cup cream until stiff. Fold into mixture. Mound high in pie shell. Refrigerate for at least 3 hours.

Topping:
Beat cream with confectioner's sugar until stiff. Pipe lattice work on pie.

Amt Measure	Ingredient — Preparation Method
4	eggs — separated
1/4 cup	cold water
1 envelope	unflavored gelatin
1/4 cup	lemon juice
1 cup	sugar
1/4 teaspoon	salt
1 tablespoon	lemon peel — grated
	yellow food coloring
1/2 cup	heavy cream
1 9-inch	graham cracker crust

Topping:

1/2 cup	heavy cream
2 tablespoons	powdered sugar

Quick Fruit Cobbler

Servings: 6 • Preheat to 350°...

Amt Measure	Ingredient — Preparation Method
1/2 cup	sugar
1/2 cup	all-purpose flour
1/2 cup	milk
1 teaspoon	baking powder
1/4 teaspoon	salt
2 cups	fresh or frozen berries

Glaze:

1/2 stick	butter or margarine
1 cup	brown sugar
1/4 cup	milk

In a bowl, combine the sugar, flour, milk, baking powder and salt.

Pour into a 9"x9" greased baking pan.

Top with berries.

Bake for 40 minutes.

While the cobbler is baking, prepare the glaze by boiling ingredients for 5 minutes.

Pour the hot glaze over the cobbler immediately after baking.

Serving Ideas:
Wonderful with scoop of vanilla ice cream.

Whitestone Chess Fruit Pie

Servings: 8 • Preheat to 300°...

Mix all ingredients together (except pie shell).

Pour into pie shell.

Bake for 45 minutes until set.

NOTE:

Excellent served warm!

Amt Measure	Ingredient — Preparation Method
4	eggs
1 1/3 cups	sugar
2/3 cup	chopped pecans
2/3 cup	coconut
2/3 cup	raisins
1 1/2 tablespoons	vinegar
1/3 pound	butter or margarine — melted
1 9-inch	pie shell — unbaked

Whitestone Delight Pie

Serving Size: 16

Amt Measure	Ingredient — Preparation Method
2 9-inch	deep dish pie shells — baked
1 stick	butter or margarine
1 cup	pecans — chopped
2 cups	coconut — grated
8 ounces	cream cheese — softened
14 ounces	sweetened condensed milk
16 ounces	whipping cream — whipped
6 ounces	caramel topping
6 ounces	chocolate syrup

Melt butter in skillet and sauté coconut and pecans until lightly browned. Cool.

In mixing bowl, beat cream cheese and milk until smooth; continue beating as you add whipped cream.

Pour 1/4 of cream cheese filling into each pie shell. Top with 1/4 of coconut/pecan mixture.

Drizzle well with caramel syrup.

Repeat layers.

Wrap pie in foil and place in freezer for at least 4 to 8 hours.

To serve:

Remove pies from freezer about 15 minutes before serving.

Cut each pie into 8 wedges.

Drizzle chocolate syrup over pie. Add additional caramel syrup if desired.

NOTE:
This is a wonderful dessert and a favorite with our guests.

Cakes

. . . **W**hitestone was exactly what we needed. A special treat, a special memory, a special gift! . . .

Henry David Thoreau said it, "If a man does not keep pace with his companions, perhaps it is because he hears a different drummer. Let him step to the music he hears, however measured or far away..." A more modern expression for such individuals is the term "visionary." Thank you, Paul and Jean, for your vision. this place was a refuge, a refreshing, a sanctuary. . . .

Amish Cake

Servings: 12 • Preheat oven to 350°...

Amt Measure	Ingredient — Preparation Method
Cake:	
2 cups	*all-purpose flour*
2 cups	*sugar*
1 teaspoon	*vanilla*
2	*eggs — beaten*
1 1/2 teaspoons	*baking soda*
20 ounces	*canned crushed pineapple with juice*
1 cup	*black walnuts — chopped*
Frosting:	
1 stick	*butter — softened*
8 ounces	*cream cheese — softened*
2 cups	*powdered sugar*
1 teaspoon	*vanilla*

Combine flour, sugar, vanilla, eggs, and baking soda until thoroughly blended.

Add crushed pineapple and black walnuts.

Bake in ungreased 9"x13" baking pan for 35 to 40 minutes until cake is deep golden color. Cool.

Cream Cheese Frosting:

Mix butter, cream cheese, powdered sugar and 1 teaspoon vanilla.

Spread on cooled cake.

Serve cool or at room temperature.

Cranberry Coffee Cake

Servings: 12 • Preheat to 350°...

Cream butter and sugar together until light and fluffy.

Add eggs, one at a time, beating thoroughly after each.

Combine flour, baking powder, baking soda and salt.

Add flour mixture to creamed mixture alternately with sour cream, beating well after each addition. Add almond extract and mix well.

Spoon half of mixture into a greased and floured 10-inch tube pan. Spread half of cranberry sauce over batter.

Repeat layers ending with cranberry sauce. Sprinkle pecans over top.

Bake for 1 hour or until cake tests done.

Let cool 5 minutes before removing from pan.

Amt Measure	Ingredient — Preparation Method
1/2 cup	butter or margarine — softened
1 cup	sugar
2	eggs
2 cups	all-purpose flour — sifted AFTER measuring
1 teaspoon	baking powder
1 teaspoon	baking soda
1/2 teaspoon	salt
1 cup	sour cream
1 teaspoon	almond extract
16 ounces	canned whole cranberry sauce
1/2 cup	pecans — chopped

Glaze:

Combine glaze ingredients and mix well. Add a little more water if needed.

Drizzle over top of coffee cake after removing from pan.

Glaze:

3/4 cup	powdered sugar — sifted
1/2 teaspoon	almond extract
3 tablespoons	warm water

Fresh Apple Cake

Servings: 15 • Preheat oven to 350°...

Amt Measure	Ingredient — Preparation Method
Cake:	
1 1/2 cups	oil
2 cups	sugar
3 large	eggs
3 cups	all-purpose flour
1 teaspoon	salt
1 teaspoon	baking soda
3 cups	apples — peeled & sliced
1 1/2 cups	walnuts — chopped

Caramel Topping:	
1 cup	light brown sugar
1 stick	margarine
1/4 cup	evaporated milk
1 teaspoon	vanilla

Mix together the oil, sugar and eggs.

Add flour, salt and soda.

Fold in the apples and nuts.

Pour into greased and floured 9"x13" pan.

Bake one hour until cake tests done.

Caramel Topping:

Over medium heat, combine the brown sugar, margarine, milk and vanilla, stirring constantly.

Cook 2 to 3 minutes.

Spoon warm topping over cake at serving time.

Heavenly Chocolate Cake

Servings: 12 • Preheat to 350°...

Mix water and cocoa. Let cool. Add margarine, sugar, eggs and vanilla.

Combine 3/4 cup flour, baking soda and baking powder. Set aside.

Combine remaining flour and salt. Add to the chocolate mixture. Add the flour, baking soda and baking powder mixture last.

Bake in three 9-inch greased and floured cake pans for 20 to 25 minutes or until cake tests done.

Filling:

In double boiler, combine chocolate and 1/4 cup whipping cream until chocolate is melted. Add the remaining whipping cream. Chill overnight.

Beat at high speed until stiff.

Frosting:

Cook butter, coke, cocoa and vanilla until hot.

Remove from heat and add powdered sugar until it is the consistency of thick gravy. *(Frosting will thicken more as it cools.)*

Beat until spreading consistency. If frosting is too thick, add a little more coke. If too thin, add more sugar.

Amt Measure	Ingredient — Preparation Method
2 cups	*boiling water*
3/4 cup	*cocoa*
2 sticks	*margarine — softened*
2 1/2 cups	*sugar*
4 large	*eggs — room temperature*
1 1/2 teaspoons	*vanilla*
2 3/4 cups	*all-purpose flour*
2 teaspoons	*baking soda*
3/4 teaspoon	*baking powder*
1/2 teaspoon	*salt*

Filling:

3 ounces	*white chocolate*
1 pint	*heavy whipping cream*

Frosting:

1 stick	*butter — melted*
1/2 cup	*coke*
3 1/2 tablespoons	*cocoa*
1 1/2 teaspoons	*vanilla*
2 pounds	*powdered sugar (approximate amount)*

Assemble cake using the filling between the layers. Frost entire cake.

Store in refrigerator until time to serve.

Italian Creme Cake

Servings: 15 • Preheat to 350°...

Amt Measure	Ingredient — Preparation Method
2 cups	sugar
5	eggs—separated
2 sticks	butter — softened
2 cups	all-purpose flour
1 teaspoon	baking soda
1 cup	buttermilk
1 cup	coconut
1/2 cup	pecans — chopped
1 teaspoon	vanilla

Cream together sugar, eggs yolks and butter.

Add flour, baking soda, buttermilk, coconut, pecans and vanilla.

Beat egg whites until stiff. Fold into cake mixture.

Pour into three greased and floured 8-inch cake pans.

Bake for 30 to 35 minutes until cakes test done.

Icing:

Ice cooled cake with cream cheese frosting on page 114.

Jam Cake

Servings: 12 • Preheat to 325°...

ix flour, baking soda, spices and salt. Set aside.

Cream butter and gradually add sugar. Beat until fluffy. Add eggs one at a time. Beat in jam.

Blend mixtures, alternating adding buttermilk and dry ingredients in four additions. Fold in walnuts.

Pour into two 9-inch greased and floured cake pans. Bake for 45 to 50 minutes.

Frosting:

Whisk brown sugar, milk, butter, molasses and salt over low heat until smooth. Cool mixture. Transfer to large bowl.

Add sugar to mixture a little at a time. Mix after each addition. Add vanilla, mixing well.

Cover and refrigerate icing until it is good spreading consistency.

Final Preparation:

Slice cakes in half. Put jam between the sliced layers. Put frosting between cake layers.

Ice top and sides of cake.

Cover and refrigerate. Let stand at room temperature 2 hours before serving.

Amt Measure	Ingredient — Preparation Method
3 cups	all-purpose flour
1 teaspoon	baking soda
1 teaspoon	cinnamon
1/2 teaspoon	cardamom
1/2 teaspoon	clovcs
1/2 teaspoon	salt
1 cup	unsalted butter — room temperature
2 cups	packed brown sugar
6 large	eggs
1 cup	seedless blackberry jam
3/4 cup	buttermilk
1 cup	walnut pieces

Frosting:

1 1/2 cups	dark brown sugar
1 cup	evaporated milk
3/4 cup	unsalted butter
1 1/2 tablespoons	molasses
1/4 teaspoon	salt
6 1/3 cups	powdered sugar — sifted
1 1/2 teaspoons	vanilla
2 cups	jam (any fruit flavor)

Molten Chocolate Cake

Servings: 2 • Preheat to 350°...

Amt Measure	Ingredient — Preparation Method
Sauce:	
16 ounces	*pitted dark sweet cherries — halved & undrained*
1/2 cup	*sugar*
1/4 cup	*brandy*
1/4 teaspoon	*cinnamon*
Cake:	
2 tablespoons	*cocoa powder*
1/4 cup	*sugar*
2 ounces	*bittersweet or semi-sweet chocolate — chopped*
1/4 cup	*unsalted butter (1/2 stick) — cut in small pieces*
2 large	*egg yolks*
1 large	*egg*
2 teaspoons	*all-purpose flour*
	powdered sugar
	fresh mint

Sauce:

Combine all the ingredients in heavy saucepan. Stir over medium heat until sugar dissolves. Simmer until sauce thickens and is reduced slightly.

Using slotted spoon, remove 1/4 cup cherries from sauce and drain well. Chop coarsely for cakes.

Cakes:

Butter two 3/4 cup ramekins or custard cups. Whisk cocoa and sugar in small bowl to blend.

Stir chocolate and butter in heavy saucepan over low heat until chocolate melts and mixture is smooth. Remove from heat.

Whisk in the cocoa mixture; add egg yolks, then whole egg and flour.

Fold in chopped cherries and divide batter between ramekins.

Bake cakes about 20 to 25 minutes until edges are set but center is still shiny and tester comes out with some wet batter.

Cut around cakes to loosen. Turn out onto plates.

Spoon sauce along sides and dust with powdered sugar. Garnish with mint.

Orange Flourless Chocolate Cake

Serving Size: 12   •   Preheat to 350°...

Melt chocolate, butter, 1/2 tablespoon orange zest and orange juice concentrate together in a double boiler; set aside.

Combine egg whites and vanilla in mixing bowl, whipping to form soft peaks.

Slowly add sugar to whipped egg whites until stiff; set aside.

To the chocolate mixture, slowly add egg yolks until all are incorporated.

Mix in 1/3 egg whites into chocolate mixture, then gently fold in rest of egg white mixture.

Using a greased and floured 9-inch spring form pan, bake in a water bath for 30 minutes.

Whip heavy cream to form soft peaks, then fold in Cointreau. Cut cake into 8 slices.

To serve, place one ounce of orange marmalade on bottom of plate.

Then place cake on plate; top with whipped cream and orange zest.

Garnish with orange sections.

Amt Measure	Ingredient — Preparation Method
1 pound	semi-sweet chocolate
1/2 pound	butter
1/2 tablespoon	orange zest
2 ounces	orange juice, frozen concentrate
10	egg whites
1/2 teaspoon	vanilla
3 tablespoons	sugar
10	egg yolks
1/2 cup	heavy cream
1 ounce	Cointreau
8 ounces	orange marmalade
16 pieces	orange zest
24 sections	orange (optional)

Orange Slice Cake

Servings: 12 • Preheat to 300°...

Amt Measure	Ingredient — Preparation Method
1/2 teaspoon	salt
1 pound	orange slice candy — cut-up
8 ounces	dates — chopped
2 cups	pecans — chopped
1 cup	coconut
1/2 cup	all-purpose flour
1 cup	butter — melted
2 cups	sugar
4	eggs
1/2 cup	buttermilk
1 teaspoon	baking soda
3 cups	all-purpose flour

Icing:

1 cup	orange juice
2 cups	powdered sugar

Combine and stir until light: salt, orange slices, dates, pecans, coconut, and 1/2 cup flour.

In separate bowl, stir together butter, sugar, eggs, buttermilk, soda and 3 cups flour. Mix well.

Combine both mixtures.

Bake in greased and floured tube pan for 2 hours.

Icing:

Mix together well the orange juice and powdered sugar.

Pour icing over hot cake so it will soak into the cake.

Red Velvet Cake

Servings: 12 • Preheat to 350°...

Cream together the margarine, sugar and eggs.

Make a paste with the food coloring and cocoa and add to the creamed mixture.

Then add the flour, salt, buttermilk and vanilla.

Add the baking soda and vinegar last.

Bake in three 9-inch, greased and floured cake pans for 30 minutes until cakes test done.

Ice cooled cake with cream cheese frosting on page 114.

Amt Measure	Ingredient — Preparation Method
3/4 cup	margarine
2 1/4 cups	sugar
3	eggs
1/4 cup	red food coloring
1/4 cup	cocoa
3 1/3 cups	all-purpose flour
1 1/2 teaspoons	salt
1 1/2 cups	buttermilk
1 1/2 teaspoons	vanilla
1 1/2 teaspoons	baking soda
1 1/2 tablespoons	vinegar

Cookies & Bars

"Being here for our company management retreat has been such a wonderful balance of business and pleasure. Our entire management team has thoroughly enjoyed your home and hospitality. Quality customer service is reflected in all you do. We leave refreshed, renewed, re-invigorated and ready to return for more? Thanks for your gracious hospitality and kindness."

Boiled Cookies

Servings: 24

Amt Measure	Ingredient — Preparation Method
2 cups	sugar
1/4 cup	butter
1/4 cup	cocoa
1/2 cup	milk
2/3 cup	peanut butter
2 cups	oatmeal — uncooked
1 teaspoon	vanilla

Bring the sugar, butter, cocoa and milk to a rolling boil and remove from heat.

Add peanut butter, oatmeal and vanilla.

Mix well and drop by rounded teaspoon on wax paper.

Let cookies dry at room temperature.

California Chews

Servings: 24 • Preheat to 375°...

Sift together dry ingredients. Cream butter with sugars until light and fluffy.

Add vanilla and eggs to butter mixture and beat well.

Stir in dry ingredients until thoroughly blended.

Mix in butterscotch chips, nuts and coconut.

Drop by rounded tablespoon onto ungreased cookie sheet.

Bake for 10 to 12 minutes or until lightly browned.

Remove from baking sheet and cool on a wire rack.

Amt Measure	Ingredient — Preparation Method
2 1/4 cups	all-purpose flour
1 teaspoon	baking soda
1 teaspoon	salt
1 cup	butter — softened
3/4 cup	granulated sugar
3/4 cup	brown sugar — packed
1 teaspoon	vanilla
2	eggs
1 12-ounce pkg	butterscotch chips
1 cup	macadamia nuts — chopped
1/2 cup	coconut — flaked

Cinnamon Spice Bars

Servings: 15 • Preheat to 350°...

Amt Measure	Ingredient — Preparation Method
1 cup	sugar
3/4 cup	oil
1/4 cup	honey
2 cups	all-purpose flour
1 teaspoon	cinnamon
1 teaspoon	baking soda
1/4 teaspoon	salt
1	egg — beaten
1 cup	nuts — chopped

Frosting:

1 cup	powdered sugar
2 tablespoons	milk
1/2 teaspoon	vanilla

Combine the sugar, oil and honey.

In a separate bowl, combine the flour, cinnamon, baking soda and salt. Combine both mixtures mixing well.

Add the egg and nuts.

Press mixture into a 9"x13" pan. Batter will be stiff so press into the corners and edges evenly.

Bake for 20 minutes.

Frosting:

Combine the powdered sugar, milk and vanilla. Frost while bars are hot.

Cut into bars when cool (if you can wait that long).

NOTES:
These are wonderful and store nicely. We often use these for coffee breaks when we have corporate groups.

Georgia Peanut Cookies

Servings: 24 • Preheat to 375°...

Cream butter with sugar and peanut butter; add vanilla and egg, beating until fluffy.

Stir in baking soda and salt.

Blend in the flour and mix until stiff dough forms.

Shape into walnut-sized balls and place on a lightly greased cookie sheet.

Press with fork, crisscross to flatten; bake for 10 minutes or until lightly browned.

Cool on rack.

Amt Measure	Ingredient — Preparation Method
1/2 cup	butter — softened
1/2 cup	brown sugar — packed
1/2 cup	smooth peanut butter
1/2 teaspoon	vanilla
1	egg
1/2 teaspoon	baking soda
1/4 teaspoon	salt
1 1/2 cups	all-purpose flour

Lemon Bars

Servings: 12 • Preheat to 350°...

Amt Measure	Ingredient — Preparation Method
Crust:	
1 3/4 cups	all-purpose flour
2/3 cup	confectioners sugar
1/4 cup	cornstarch
3 3/8 teaspoons	salt
12 tablespoons	unsalted butter
Filling:	
4 large	eggs — beaten slightly
1 1/3 cups	granulated sugar
3 tablespoons	all-purpose flour
2 teaspoons	finely grated zest from 2 large lemons
2/3 cup	lemon juice (3 to 4 large lemons) — strained
1/3 cup	whole milk
1/8 teaspoon	salt
	confectioners sugar to garnish

Crust:

Lightly butter a 9x13 inch baking dish and line with parchment or wax paper.

Dot paper with butter; lay second sheet crosswise over it. (Leave edges sticking up above the edges of the dish.)

In a food processor, pulse the flour, sugar, cornstarch and salt.

Add butter and process to blend; pulse until mixture is pale yellow and resembles coarse meal.

Sprinkle mixture into lined pan; press it out to spread over bottom of the dish and 1/2 inch up the sides.

Refrigerate for 30 minutes. Reduce heat to 325° and bake for 20 minutes until golden brown.

Filling:

Whisk eggs, sugar and flour in medium bowl. Stir in remaining ingredients and blend well. Pour filling into warm crust.

Bake until filling feels firm when touched lightly (about 20 minutes).

Cool in refrigerator overnight.

To serve: Grasp the edges of the lengthwise paper and lift the bars onto a cutting board. Fold the paper down, and cut into serving size bars, wiping knife between cuts.

Sprinkle lightly with confectioners sugar to serve.

Lemon Meltaways

Servings: 24 • Preheat to 350°...

Amt Measure	Ingredient — Preparation Method
Cookies:	
1 1/4 cups	*all-purpose flour*
1/2 cup	*cornstarch*
1/3 cup	*powdered sugar*
3/4 cup	*butter — softened*
1 teaspoon	*lemon zest*
1 tablespoon	*lemon juice*
Frosting:	
3/4 cup	*powdered sugar*
1/4 cup	*butter — softened*
1 teaspoon	*lemon zest*
1 teaspoon	*lemon juice*

Combine all cookie ingredients in a mixing bowl and beat on low speed until well mixed.

Divide dough in half, then shape each half into 8"x1" roll. Wrap in plastic food wrap and refrigerate until firm—1 to 2 hours.

With a sharp knife, cut each half into 1/4 inch slices.

Place 2 inches apart on cookie sheet. Bake for 8 to 12 minutes or until set. *(Cookies will not brown.)*

Cool completely.

In a small mixer bowl, combine all frosting ingredients and beat at medium speed until fluffy. Frost cooled cookies.

Molasses Cookies

Servings: 24 • Preheat to 375°...

Amt Measure	Ingredient — Preparation Method
3/4 cup	shortening
1 cup	sugar
1/4 cup	molasses
1	egg
2 cups	all-purpose flour
2 teaspoons	baking soda
1/2 teaspoon	salt
1 teaspoon	ginger
1/2 teaspoon	cloves
1 teaspoon	cinnamon
2 cups	granulated sugar

Melt shortening over low heat; then let cool.

Add sugar, molasses, and egg; beat well.

Sift together flour, soda, salt, ginger, cloves and cinnamon.

Combine both mixtures mixing well.

Chill.

Form into 1" balls and roll in granulated sugar. (Do not flatten the balls.)

Bake 2" apart on greased cookie sheet.

Bake 8 to 10 minutes.

Whitestone

Orange Slice Cookies

Servings: 24 • Preheat to 375°...

Combine brown sugar and shortening until fluffy.

Add eggs one at a time while mixing.

Add remaining ingredients until combined.

Place on a greased cookie sheet in 1-inch balls.

Bake for 10 to 15 minutes.

Amt Measure	Ingredient — Preparation Method
2 cups	brown sugar
1 cup	shortening
3	eggs
1 teaspoon	vanilla
1 teaspoon	baking soda
1 teaspoon	cream of tartar
3 cups	all-purpose flour
18 large	orange slice candy — cut into pieces
1 cup	nuts — chopped

Peanut Butter Oatmeal Cookies

Servings: 24 • Preheat to 350°...

Amt Measure	Ingredient — Preparation Method
3/4 cup	butter flavored shortening
1 cup	peanut butter
1 1/2 cups	brown sugar — packed
1/2 cup	water
1	egg
1 teaspoon	vanilla
3 cups	oatmeal — uncooked
1 1/2 cups	all-purpose flour
1/2 teaspoon	baking soda
	granulated sugar for dipping

Beat shortening, peanut butter and brown sugar until creamy.

Beat in water, egg and vanilla.

Combine oatmeal, flour and baking soda.

Combine the two mixtures together.

Cover and chill about 2 hours.

Shape into one inch balls and place on ungreased cookie sheet.

Flatten with fork dipped in granulated sugar to form crisscross pattern.

Bake 9 to 11 minutes or until edges are golden brown.

Cool one minute on cookie sheet and remove to wire rack and cool completely.

Whitestone

Notes

Notes

Notes